Waterloo Sunrise

Discovering the past, the life and the wildlife of Katesgrove

Edited by Julie Wickham and Mike Cox

Researched by Mike Cox, Julie Wickham, Karyn Trowbridge, Lorna Grigg and Rita Brown

Published by The Katesgrove Community Book Project

Design by Julian Humphries
Illustrations by Jan Tait
Additional design by Martin Willoughby

This book couldn't have been written without the contributions of the local people listed on pages *v–vi*; people who have lived in this area for many years. We are indebted to them.

Maps and photographs courtesy of Ordnance Survey, Reading Borough Libraries, Reading University Museum of English Rural Life, Berkshire Records Office, Reading Evening Post, Reading Chronicle.

A special thank you to Graham Parlour for allowing us to use his photographs. Thank you also for photographs to Michael Barnes, John Griffin, Betty Patterson, Audrey and Ernest Bowles, Mike Cox, Val Wicks, Lorna Grigg. Thank you to Mrs Thom for allowing us to use her mother's (Phoebe Cusden's) work. Thank you to Eric Starmer.

Thank you for advice and help from Two Rivers Press and Corridor Press.

We have been supported by Reading Borough Council, Thames Print, The Earley Charity and Reading Local History Trust.

Printed by Richfield Graphics Ltd.
65, Loverock Road, Reading, Berkshire.

Dedicated to volunteers everywhere who work hard to ensure the future of important open space and habitat. Dedicated in particular to John Bassett and Jan Cox for their support and patience with this project. Also in memory of three of our contributors, Richard Johnson, William Newport and Percy Thatcher whose contributions have formed significant parts of this book and who sadly died whilst it was being written.

The following song, '*Tales from the River Bank*' was written by Paul Weller and was recorded by the Jam in 1981. It sums up some of our feelings about Waterloo Meadows, the place that brought us all together, and the reason why we wrote this book.

Bring you a tale from the pastel fields
Where we ran when we were young
This is a tale from the Water Meadows,
Trying to spread some hope into your heart.

It's mixed with happiness it's mixed with tears,
Both life and death got married in this dream,
That open space you can run for miles,
Now you don't get so many to the pound.

True it's a dream mixed with nostalgia,
But it's a dream that I'll always hang on to,
That I'll always run to,
Won't you join me by the river bank.

Many thanks to Mr Paul Weller for his permission to use the song

Foreword

'I have read 'Waterloo Sunrise' with great interest. I have found it an absolutely fascinating book to read, full of interesting facts from first class accounts by local people who have spent most of their life in and around the Katesgrove area. With such anecdotes as the man that used to sell muffins door to door and the man that sold bananas at 14 for a penny, the stories and the wildlife there, it is a book that once you start to read , you are reluctant to put it down.'

Harold Hill, *Reading Evening Post*

Introduction

Waterloo Meadows was the place that brought the five authors and the contributors together. It is the area of open space bordered by Elgar Road South, Rose Kiln Lane and the River Kennet. I had lived in Katesgrove six months and I didn't know that there was a place called Waterloo Meadows. Then I got a letter through the door from a group called the 'Friends of Waterloo Meadows'. The Kennet Meadows needed help. There was a threat to build on them and outline planning permission had been sought. I felt so strongly that I joined the group and the rest, as they say, is history. We decided that the book should have three elements:

Oral history: Recollections from people who had lived in the area all their lives.

History and research Just what was this area that we lived in: What had it been in its past?

The meadows: A natural history

I wanted to celebrate what was there now and say...this is on your doorstep, value what's there or you'll lose it. I visited the meadows every month to document the wildlife, and write about the other creatures that shared this space with us. The last section of the book may seem separate from the rest but we hope you'll agree, it's probably the bit that gives the rest its raison d'être. Read on and enjoy...

Julie Wickham, March 1999

How does this book work?

To save repeating the names of our contributors we have given each of them a symbol. You will find the symbol next to their names on the following pages. Whenever you see their symbol you will know who is talking.

Sid Ballard   Born 1920. Worked for 15 years at Robert Corts engineering works.

Dave Ballard   Was a child in the 50's and has lived in the Katesgrove area all his life.

Rita Brown   Rita lives in Elgar road, and has lived in the area for most of her life.

Eric Cooper   Aged 87 at the time of going to press. Worked at the CO-OP preserve works for two years as assistant engineer. Has lived in the area all his life. Was an apprentice in Lynn Street for a cabinet makers.

Mike Cox   Was a child in the 60's and has lived in the Katesgrove area for most of his life.

Wilf Fewtrell   Born approx. 1928. Was about 9 in 1937.

David Geary   Started work at the CO-OP printing works in 1966 and worked there for 15 years. Was Mayor when we first interviewed him.

Joan Hobbs   Moved to Swainstone Road in 1939 and lived there until approx. 1986.

Richard Johnson   Lived in Milman Road from 1914/15 until 1938. Aged approx. 86 in 1996.

Bob Legge   Has lived in the area for many years.

William Newport Worked at Waterloo Meadows Landfill Site in the 50's.

 Fred Paintin Born 6th January 1918, has Lived in Elgar Road all his life.

 Edna and Les Plested Edna worked at the CO-OP in the 1950's. Lived in Elgar Road from 1935 until 1953. She was 3 when she first moved there and stayed until she was 18 when she got married.

 Arthur Sayer Aged 75 in 1996. Has lived in Collis Street nearly all his life.

 Percy Thatcher Employed by the CO-OP printing works in 1936 and retired in 1976.

 Sheila Trenchard Worked at the CO-OP.

 Dolly and Percy Warrick Percy worked at the CO-OP printing works from 1955/56 until just before it closed.

 Ann Weight Born in Collis Street in 1943. Lived there until 1977.

 Ann's Mother Ann's Mother was born in 1915 and moved away approx. 1994.

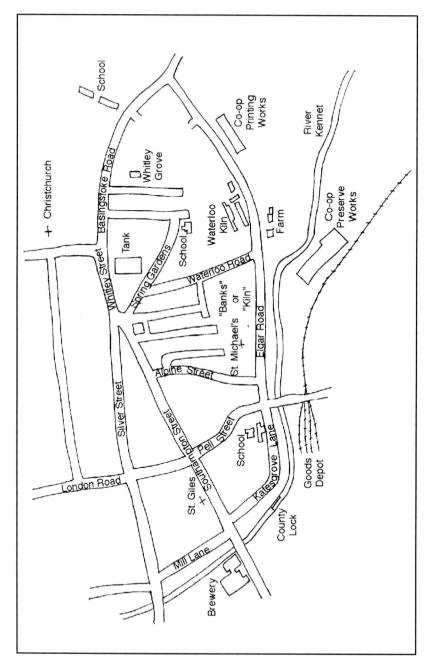

Diagram showing approximate locations of places refered to in this book, based on OS map

Contents

Reading from the South Hill - London Illustrated News

Waterloo Sunrise

Chapter One
An Overview of Katesgrove from 1643 - 1931
Compiled from Historical Maps

Katesgrove itself had very humble beginnings. It appears to have been the next area developed after the main town was established. It was effectively the first industrial estate of the town, and was from the start a very poor area. The hovels next to St. Giles' church can be remembered by people, even today. St Giles was the patron saint of beggars. This poverty lasted until recent times, and there are still parts of Katesgrove that are not that well off. However, the area has thrived, and as will be seen in the following pages, has had quite a history .

It is difficult to chart the history of an area over many years. Much of our information is incomplete and fragmentary but with careful study you begin to get a feel for an area's heritage.

In 1643 the Kennet Meadows were called 'Drounde Meadows'. Trees lined the banks of the river. The town wall at this time ran right through the area we know today as Waterloo Meadows; there was a small copse there, too.

The area was clearly rich in clay and by 1802 the first Brick Kiln had appeared. It belonged to a Mr Waugh and was situated on the East side of Elgar Road, roughly where Tippett Rise is now. The Brick Kiln had its own set of buildings. It was divided up into small fields with evidence of cultivation. Whitley was just a small hamlet at the top of Southampton Street with a turnpike. A mysterious feature that appeared on maps at this time was Bob's Mount and it overlooked the brick kiln. South of the kilns there was an area known as Clackman or Clerkenwell fields.

There was clearly a farm or manor at the top of Southampton Street with substantial buildings and cultivation.

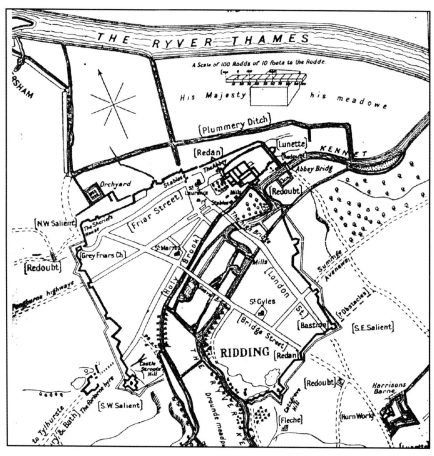

Map of 1643

The following accounts from tell us a little of what life was like in the early 19th century, ending with the sad account of the death of Alderman Blandy.

From "Reading 70 years ago" a record of events from 1813 to 1819 - P. H.

Ditchfield

May 23 1816

The parish officers of St. Giles, with some of the inhabitants, perambulated the bounds of the parish; they set off from the Bear Meadow at 9 o'clock and arrived at Whitley Farm, which is occupied by Mr Frankland, one of the overseers, at 1 o'clock, where they sat down to an excellent dinner of veal and ham and pigeon pie, with good appetites, after which they sailed down the Kennet to the place they set off from, and having regaled 11 boys (who accompanied them) with bread and cheese and beer, at the Little Crown, and gave them a shilling each, they repaired to the Crown Inn, where they closed the day.

July 19 1816

The weather still continues wet; the farmers are taking up the clover hay and throwing it on the dung-hill. The Kennet and Loddon meadows are all flooded.

December 23 1816

This year has not added much in size to our town. Five more houses have been built in Clackman Field by Mr Harris, but to the number of paupers and the distress of those already so, there has been great addition; the pawnbroker's shop is the one most frequented by those who have any property besides the clothes upon them; those who have not are in a most wretched state; bread and vegetables constitute the chief of their food, and of this they are obliged to eat sparingly; sometimes some of them buy a pennyworth of bullocks liver, but as there is not much beef killed, this is a luxury all cannot obtain.

26 January 1817

The labouring men of St. Giles' parish who apply to the overseers for relief, are now employed in opening a gravel pit in Clackman Field.

18 December 1817

This morning Alderman Wm. Blandy went to the bathing house in Katesgrove to bathe, according to his usual custom, and was drowned.

In 1840 the area remained much the same with the addition of another

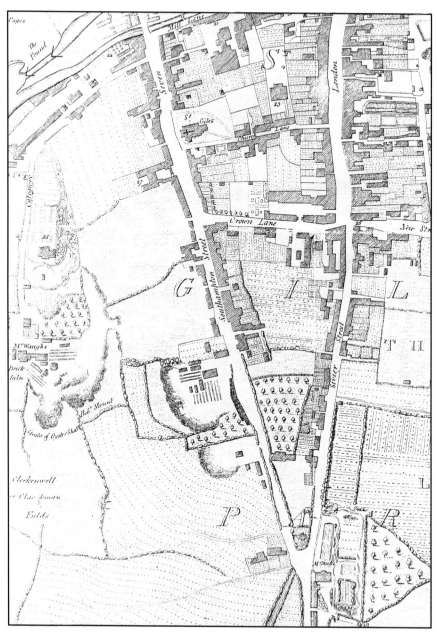

Charles Tompkins Map (1802)

Brick Kiln. Katesgrove House appeared in Katesgrove Lane and is still there today next to the school. There was an unmade road leading from one of the Brick Kilns through the farmstead buildings to the top of Southampton Street.

The Tithe Map of 1841

The Tithe Map of 1841 is very revealing. In it the Meadows are labelled simply as Land Mead which translates roughly from the Germanic as mowed land. Waterloo Kiln is named Waterloo for the first time. The Kiln also had its own "cut" presumably for transporting the bricks from the kiln via the river to the canal. At the junction of the cut and the river there was a "Withey Eyot" which was used for growing Osiers. Osiers were reeds used for thatch, baskets and wicker work. This would have been approximately at the end of Elgar Road north side just before where the Children's Centre is today. It was owned in 1841 by Baronet George Milman and was rented to George Shackel.

At this time the Meadow was largely owned by three people – Sir William George Milman (Baronet), the Reverend Brown and the Reverend Frederick Gardiner, the first owning the lion's share.

George Shackel featured as a prominent tenant farmer. In addition to renting the "Withey Eyot" he also occupied a sizeable market garden and ran the cricket field. The rest of the land, other than Waterloo Kiln was cultivated meadow land rented by different tenant farmers and there were two "homesteads" in the kiln area.

By 1861 Waterloo Road was named and there had been a flurry of development at the top of Southampton Street. 1879 saw the first horse-drawn tram in Reading (C Norman Evening Post). From the maps we can see that the Coley area also had a kiln on the Coley Park Estate. Despite the increase in transport much of the area was still divided into fields and meadows.

By 1872 – 1877 substantial development had occurred. A reservoir, owned by Reading Waterworks was situated near Whitley Street. The Katesgrove Kiln Company had dug a new Brick Field. Waterloo Kilns are shown on the map as making brick tiles and drainpipes. Rose Kiln brick and tile works is also shown, very near to Fobney Meadow. This map also marks the appearance of Christchurch School (for boys, girls and infants) and a Weslyan Methodist Chapel very near to the reservoir. In addition there appears to be a great increase in the building of terraced housing, perhaps related to the increase in brick and tile works in the area but mainly to house the workers of Reading's large industries.

The following is taken from census information at Reading Local Studies Library. It allows us to compare the difference in occupations over the forty years from 1851 - 1891.

1851 - People who lived at Park Place, Waterloo Road;

Milliner
5 laundresses
Cattle dealer employing 1 man
Dress maker

Book maker
2 shoebinders
Attorney's general clerk
Grocer's porter
Baker
Brickmaker
3 agricultural labourers
2 charwomen
3 domestic servants
Gardener
Brickmaker's labourer
Cordwainer
Dairyman's labourer
Gardener's labourer
Dairyman's boy

People were mainly working either for themselves or for very small concerns, or were in domestic service. There were not many large employers at the time, although the Iron Works in Katesgrove Lane actually employed 250 people.

The Whitley Street Area had some grand sounding residences on it at this time - Highclere Villas, Kingsclere Villas, Ivy Lodge, Belgrave Cottage, Whitley Lodge, but for all the increase in terraced housing, Whitley Street was still largely surrounded by fields and trees.

1891 - People who lived in Elgar Road:

Turner and fitter
2 Bakers - biscuit factory
5 labourers - biscuit factory
Dock porter
French polisher
Tailoress
Compositor
Postman

Tinsmith
2 Tinworkers
2 Labourers – water works
Brewer's dreyman
Railway porter
Engine driver
Labourer – coal yard
Wood sawyer
3 carpenters
Groom
Clerk
3 policemen
Shoemaker
General labourer
3 brickmakers
Dairyman
Grocer
Smith – iron works

By comparison to 1851 it is clear that more people were working for larger organisations.

By 1911 Rose Kilns were disused. Whereas Rose Kilns had been situated near the River Kennet, Whitley Kiln (brick works) was located between the River Kennet and the Basingstoke Road, half way down what is now Cradock Road. Waterloo Kilns (brick and tile works) was situated on the Whitley Street side of Elgar Road. In the years between 1877 and 1911 there was much development. There was a great deal of terraced housing between Whitley Street and Elgar Road: Collis Street, Lynn Street, Spring Gardens, Essex Street, Milman Road and Swainstone Road had all been built. The land between Elgar Road and these houses was taken up with meadow land and then beyond that with allotment gardens. This ties in with the memories of local people that there were allotments on both sides of Waterloo Road. The whole area after the kilns had gone was referred to as "the banks". By 1931 Whitley Kiln was disused. Rose Kiln was referred to as Old Kilns but Waterloo Kilns (brick and tile works) were still apparently in use.

It seems that a whole area grew up around the Katesgrove brickworks, and whomever they were owned by at various times. An area that was largely

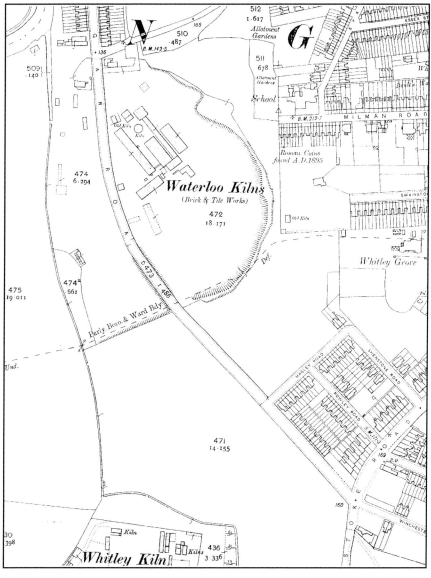

OS (1911)

farmland, trees and country estates changed over the course of a century into a built up area with houses for workers and other amenities which such a community would need.

Chapter Two – Industry in the Area

In the following section we take a closer look at the industry of the area. We have tried to place it loosely in chronological order. We have taken our information from a variety of sources and as the history gets more recent we have documented oral histories from local people.

Sailcloth

'The Growth of Reading' 1993, edited by Malcolm Petyt says that 'civic and industrial innovations were speeded up by the external shock of the revolutionary and Napoleonic wars from 1793 onwards. As an inland town, Reading provided not only agricultural but also military supplies of many kinds. Musgrave Lamb's sailcloth factory, in 'Reading's industrial estate', manufactured so much sailcloth for the Royal Navy that the Battle of Trafalgar was said to have been won in Katesgrove Lane!'

'The cloth, noted for its strength and whiteness, was greatly in demand by both the Royal Navy and The East India Company. Production was started in 1640, and flourished to such an extent, that by 1816 no fewer then 140 looms were involved'.

The Iron Works

At one time there were several iron works in Katesgrove. The biggest of these was also situated in Katesgrove Lane, and extended across the river, with its own bridge. This was the only bridge crossing the river at the time; the road bridge at Berkeley Avenue was not built until later.

The Iron Works occupied some 12 acres. The following information is summarised from the sale catalogue in the local studies library. Buildings on the site included: foundries, a warehouse, bar iron store, turnery, smithy, erecting shop, engine house, a grindery, a showroom, a wood machinery shop, boiler making shed, a pattern loft, paint shed, range of saw pits, timber shed, and offices. There were large yards, a cart yard with covered sheds, a nag stable, coach house, chaff-cutting house and a corn store, with a hay loft over it. There was also a large area of meadow land, which was used for hay and grazing purposes. Traction engines were one of the most important products.

'Reading Iron Works Limited' as it was called, went into liquidation in 1888. It was sold at auction, and was described in the sales catalogue as follows: 'For nearly 100 years (these buildings have been) occupied as one of the Principal Engineering Establishments in the Country'.

'The construction of the railway in 1840, to link London with Bath and

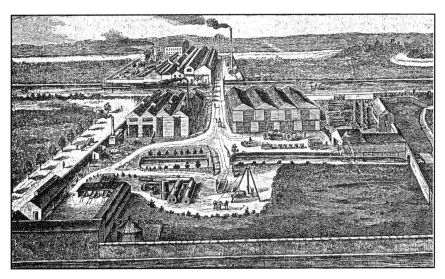

The Reading Iron Works

Bristol, helped to bring prosperity to a small foundry in Katesgrove Lane, from which materials were purchased locally. The foundry later became the Reading Iron Works, one of the largest suppliers of agricultural machinery in Britain with 360 employees. Though in the forefront of contemporary technology, especially steam engines, the iron works failed in 1887 through commercial incompetence, during the prolonged agricultural slump which had begun in the 1870's. But for this mismanagement, Katesgrove Lane might have added to its Trafalgar fame by later housing one of the most important engineering works in the south of England'. (Petyt 1993)

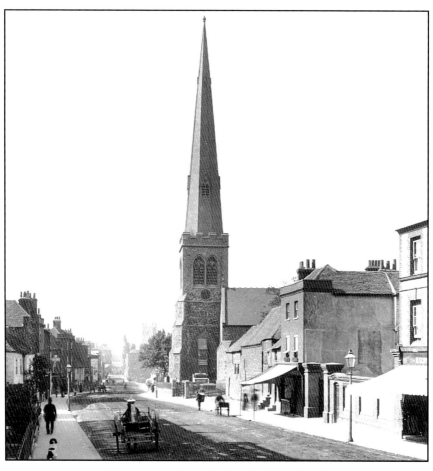

Southampton Street, showing St. Giles Church

The Brick Kilns

Perhaps one of the most significant industries for the Katesgrove area was brick and tile making. We have already noted the development of the brick kilns and clay pits in the information we have gleaned from historical maps but we will now look at them in greater detail and at what it was like to work in them or live next door to them.

One impact that the brick kilns undoubtedly had on the Reading area as a whole was that they formed the building material for much of Victorian Reading. Mr Waugh's Kiln was later known as Katesgrove Kiln. Local knowledge tells us that St Michael's Church was built on the site of it, and in more recent years the building became the Glossifilm factory. It was demolished several years ago to make way for Dale Road and Tippett Rise flats which are there now.

Waterloo Kiln was further along Elgar Road, on the bend of the road, where the industrial estate is now, and where the Robert Cort site was. It seems to have been the biggest kiln in the area, and was in use for many years.

William Newport worked for Solly Joel who owned a huge estate on the Earley side of Reading. He tells us,

> I used to drive for Mr Poulton. He owned Waterloo Kiln and sold it in 1908. I think he built a lot of houses in Elgar Road including the boathouse and number 56. I used to pick up Mr Poulton and three or four others and take them to Lambourn. Mr Poulton was Solly Joel's friend as was Mr Bailey a big grocer in Reading and Mr Bradley of Bliss printers. I had to go in the kitchens of hotels and pubs with the other drivers. I never went in with Solly Joel and his friends.

Later the kiln was known as Colliers. The following is an extract from 'Men of the Period' (Biographical Publishing Company):
'Increasing industrial activity has been a marked feature of the progress of Reading in modern times, and in this connection a prominent place

is taken by the firm of Messrs. Poulton and Son, to whose extensive business, carried on at the Adamantine Brick Works (Waterloo Kiln), attaches a record of over half a century's successful development. This firm was founded in 1850 by the late Mr. John Poulton, and is controlled today by his son, Mr. Councillor William Poulton, JP, who is also one of Reading's prominent public men.

The renown of Messrs. Poulton and Sons is far-reaching. Their products are sent to all parts of the world, and to meet demand for them the Works have been extended until they occupy a property of 46 acres, with immense productive capacity.

Well situated on the banks of the Kennet, these works have excellent transport facilities by way of that river, in conjunction with the canal and the Thames; and the firm are thus enabled to make prompt delivery of goods to any point. The manufacture is carried on under the best modern conditions, with the aid of much improved machinery, and a high reputation is maintained for machine-made building bricks, sand-faced facing bricks, silver-grey facing bricks, red roofing tiles, red ridge tiles, chimney pots, moulded bricks, and red brick enrichments. Poulton's Patent Curvilinear Boiler Seating Blocks and Flue Covers were also made.

Councillor Poulton is, not only a businessman whose energy and ability are strongly evident, but also a public worker, in which connection he has distinguished himself by good service to the Town of Reading. He entered the Town Council in 1886, and was elected Mayor of the Borough in 1899, an office he filled with notable tact and ability'.

Local knowledge tells us that Mr Poulton lived in Milman Road in one of the big houses, called Kingsclere. His father-in-law was a Mr Swain who lived at another of the big houses, Highclere. (This became the house where the 'Home Children' lived, which is mentioned elsewhere in this book.) Mr Swain was a local businessman, who had a premises in Broad Street, and whose family ran a well-known brush and rope making business in Minster Street for many years. He had an interest in Waterloo Kiln, and used this interest to provide the bricks to build the houses in a new road, next to Milman Road. This was named after him - Swainstone Road.

Waterloo Kiln initially only had a track to serve it, - the bricks were hauled up the hill by horse and cart to Whitley Street. This track was clearly very useful and became Waterloo Road. Elgar Road was extended eventually so that it joined up with the Basingstoke Road. A wharf was also built to serve the kiln.

A large house was built on the corner of Waterloo Road and Elgar Road. It served as a Caretaker-Manager's house, offices and as a builders merchants.

Fred Paintin remembers:

'We could see the men in the pit digging out the clay with spades. This was loaded onto wheelbarrows and was then taken for stacking, across a succession of planks balanced on upturned barrels or wooden boxes. A relay of men did this job. One passed the full load to the next, took an empty and returned to the point he came from'.

Sid Ballard remembers these planks:

'What was good fun, we used to get into the brick kiln, and we used to run across the planks. As you can imagine, they bounced well as the men ran across, and banged. We were actually warned to keep away, as there was a certain amount of sludge underneath the planks, which we used to go smack into'.

Wilf Fewtrell recalls:

'The clay was made into the shape of bricks, and was put into trays. These were stacked in the drying sheds, which were open sided, so the wind could blow through. They were like cycle-racks. We knew a family that had just had a baby. The husband worked at the clay pits. I remember him coming home every Thursday, wondering if he had got the

Workers outside Waterloo Kiln. This house was on the corner of Waterloo Road and Elgar Road

sack because of the bad weather. When it rained significantly, they were not allowed to go over the planks because the clay was too muddy. He would come home filthy. It wasn't like the mines; they didn't have pithead baths. I remember that there were storage yards at the kiln - it was a very big place'.

Eric Cooper recalls:

'Francis Street was built with bricks from there. When the bricks were being fired in the kilns, you could not put your washing out because of the smuts. Gwilliams Kiln was down off where Cradock Road is now. My uncle was a bricklayer, and he worked on a lot of the houses that Mr Gwilliam owned, using bricks from his kiln. He owned a lot of houses around here. The other kiln in the area was Mr Rose's. This was Rose Kiln and was down by the river, where the Rose Kiln Lane Bridge is now. This is where Rose Kiln Lane gets its name'. Waterloo Kiln was closed in the late 1940's.'

The Co-op

As the importance of the kilns diminished, two of the biggest employers in the area became the Co-op Preserve Works and the Co-op Printing Works. The Co-op Printing Works was in Elgar Road and opened in 1933. It was originally intended that it would employ four hundred people, but actual numbers reached between seven and eight hundred.

Percy Thatcher was employed by the Co-op in 1936 and was there for forty years.

'When it first opened, you could not get a job there. The master printers locally put a ban on taking their employees. There were a lot of small printing firms locally and if they'd been allowed to take them there wouldn't have been any staff left. You can't blame them in a way. It took about three or four years before they lifted it and would allow locals to go up there. Consequently when we went there to work all the foremen were from Manchester or Newcastle, sometimes Southampton, anywhere, all over the country. The top jobs were mopped up by people out of town.'

Percy finished up as Head Reader in the reading room.

'In 1936 it (the works) was extended to the side and the rear. By the time the extensions were completed, the war had broken out, and the back bit of the building was taken over by the American Army. That was when the Americans came in to the war.

As well as printing, there was a pyjama factory, which also made shirts. It was over in one corner, that was the Basingstoke Road corner of it. It employed 70 girls. It was properly called the Mantle factory, and was evacuated from London during the war. After the war, the area was taken back over for printing. There was also a flour factory which made blancmange.

The printing that was done was not all just for the Co-op, but obviously a large amount was - magazines, posters, jam and pickle labels, accounts and balance sheets, vouchers, and Christmas catalogues. They made cartons, bags for corn, sugar bags, and paper bags by the thousand to serve the Co-op shops. They also made tubes for sweets, and cardboard bottle-top discs. The kids used to play with these; the card was thick and of different colours. They played a game like Tiddlywinks'.

David Geary worked at the Co-op printing works in 1966 and worked there for 15 years.

 'They also made foolscap paper, and cash books. They used to do gold lettering and old-style ledger books. They had beautiful colouring - marbling. Everything was bound in leather'.

Edna Plested worked at the Co-op in the 1950's. One of her first jobs was working in the book-binding department.

 'There were all sorts there - wirers, gatherers, people sewing, people doing the binding.

Sheila Trenchard remembers:

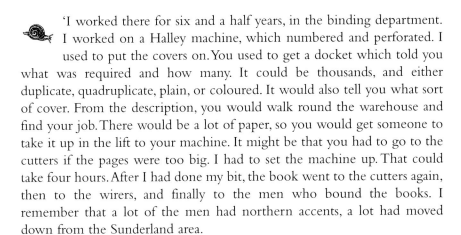

'I worked there for six and a half years, in the binding department. I worked on a Halley machine, which numbered and perforated. I used to put the covers on. You used to get a docket which told you what was required and how many. It could be thousands, and either duplicate, quadruplicate, plain, or coloured. It would also tell you what sort of cover. From the description, you would walk round the warehouse and find your job. There would be a lot of paper, so you would get someone to take it up in the lift to your machine. It might be that you had to go to the cutters if the pages were too big. I had to set the machine up. That could take four hours. After I had done my bit, the book went to the cutters again, then to the wirers, and finally to the men who bound the books. I remember that a lot of the men had northern accents, a lot had moved down from the Sunderland area.

We used to do the Co-op Home Magazine there. There was an under-foreman who sat up high, and would watch the women working. He would tell you off if you were not quick enough. We all sat in rows'.

David Geary was a reader; he corrected what other people had typed. He recalls 'You had to have a good knowledge of spelling and grammar, doing that job'.

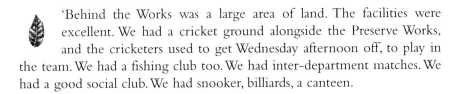

'Behind the Works was a large area of land. The facilities were excellent. We had a cricket ground alongside the Preserve Works, and the cricketers used to get Wednesday afternoon off, to play in the team. We had a fishing club too. We had inter-department matches. We had a good social club. We had snooker, billiards, a canteen.

Immediately after the war they laid two tennis courts. They laid the foundations themselves, then had somebody in to do the top surface. When we got a bit older, some of the men wanted a bowling green, so we made one by the side. It was a superb green, one of the best in the town. Frank King, the chief maintenance worker, built a pavilion, and tended to the beautiful garden with cherry blossom and almond blossom that we had.

When the site was sold they were all dug up.

'I used to ride my bike to work, and go home, and get changed, and go back in the evening to play tennis or bowls. In 1950 we couldn't get enough cars to play an away game – we used to walk or go by bike. But by about 1965 they all got cars , one by one'.

'We had a big children's party, and there was always a Christmas party on the Friday before Christmas. We had a big Christmas tree and all the workers took in a present, which was given to charity'.

'The Co-op was a good employer. We had a clinic, with 2 nurses. There was a laundry at the Preserve Factory. They had their own fire-brigade, too. That was quite common in those days'.

The Co-op Printing Works, Reading. 2

The Co-op Preserve Works (or The Jam Factory)

The Co-op Preserve works was more commonly known as the Jam Factory. It was built on land between the Kennet and the Holy Brook, and was opened in 1919.

> Leslie North (Reading Chronicle 28/10/94) tells us:
> 'When the factory was newly completed in 1916, it was taken over for what became famed as the Royal Flying Corps No 1 School of Instruction, formed a year previously, for the training of 500 fitters and riggers, and also 300 officers. Coley House became the headquarters.

> Flying training was given in the field alongside the River Kennet, and lessons in aerial recognisance, at Reading University's Wantage Hall. By 1917, the town had hundreds of Corps members billeted under canvas in Coley Park. In April 1918, the Royal Flying Corps amalgamated with the Royal Naval Air Service to form the Royal Air Force'.

> 'To begin with the 'jam factory' only made jam although later they went on to make pickles, sauces and mincemeat. The Jam factory used to smell of lemon curd always on the days when it made lemon curd. The factory had days when it made only one product'.

> Co-op Literature tells us:
> 'Fruit came in from South, East, and West, and from overseas via Southampton. The factory had its own railway siding, which meant that trucks could pull up alongside, so handling was kept to a minimum. 48 steam-jacketed pans were at boiling point all day, turning picked fruit and sugar into jam. There were low chambers into which the jam could be run to be cooled, and from which, on little tram lines, the jam was run to the packers. There was machinery for washing jars, and a machine for affixing labels. This machine made a stone weight of paste go as far as a hundredweight in ordinary use. Twelve thousand gross of empty jars (approx. 1,728,000), were filled with jam, and the new patent canning machinery (cutting out the use of solder), meant that the stockrooms were piled high. (Co-op 1996)

Eric Cooper worked at the jam factory. He was assistant to the Chief Engineer. He said:

 '...the super-heated steam was used for making pie-fillings, as well as jam. The yard was full of barrels, with the fruit in, or onions, perhaps'.

Dolly said her mum worked there during the war:

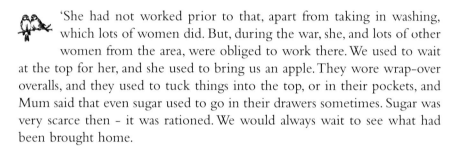 'She had not worked prior to that, apart from taking in washing, which lots of women did. But, during the war, she, and lots of other women from the area, were obliged to work there. We used to wait at the top for her, and she used to bring us an apple. They wore wrap-over overalls, and they used to tuck things into the top, or in their pockets, and Mum said that even sugar used to go in their drawers sometimes. Sugar was very scarce then - it was rationed. We would always wait to see what had been brought home.

The story was, that sometimes, when the workers came out, and they saw police at the end, they knew it was search-time, and threw all they had in the river'. The works closed in 1968.

The Tanyard

Leather was produced at Filberts Tannery in Katesgrove Lane. This was known as the Tanyard. It employed many men from the area, and the leather they produced was of the best quality. Fred Paintin said that it was a great attraction to the kids in the area to watch the men heave the hides out of the pits that were full of bark liquid, then watching them scrape the hair off, using a tool like a spokeshave.

Mr Johnson:

 The tannery smelt very strongly. There were houses on the opposite side of the road which were of the old fashioned type overhanging the road. The lane was quite narrow then. The smell from the

Working with hides at a tannery

tannery was terrible and the skins hung over the lane. The houses behind have all been knocked down now but those roads were poor. You were lucky if you walked down them without having your throat cut.'

Many people remember the awful smell of the Tannery.

'The Tanyard was a large wooden building. Denton's yard was next door to it. Dentons used to live in a house by the yard. Our house was one of a group of houses that were also next to the Tanyard, but on the other side. Pilgrim's yard was next to us. They had horses and carts. They were a removals firm. He also had a lorry. He was a very big man, smart man, with a suit and waistcoat, and a watch chain across his chest. He always wore a bowler hat. My brother worked at the Tanyard, and possibly my father, but I don't remember that. It was destroyed by a fire, and possibly the cottages opposite'.

There was a tannery in Katesgrove Lane as late as the 1950's and early 1960's.

Simond's Brewery

The drayman's cart at Simond's Brewery

24

This was situated in Bridge Street and alongside Fobney Street. It was a huge site, and was one of Reading's foremost industries. Fred Paintin's father worked on the loading bay, as a checker, so far as he knew. He went to work very early, came home to breakfast, and then went back to work until Midday, then home.

'In Fobney Street were the stables for the horses. I don't know how I found out they were there, but more than once I was found down there looking at them, and someone had to bring me home'.

Les' father worked there, with the horses. He was kicked in the stomach by one of them, and was killed.

Joan Hobbs worked all her working life for the brewery. She got a job there straight from school, because her sister was already working there. She remembers her boss, Mr Hawkes. He was the General Manager.

'He had a white handlebar moustache, and always wore a bowler hat and a buttonhole. He was known to be a hard boss. During the war, one of the staff came into work without stockings, and he told her off, even though stockings were rationed then'.

Milling

The Domesday Book tells us that Reading had 4 mills. One or more must have been where Mill Lane now runs. The Kennet at that point was made up of many streams, hence Seven Bridges House. As early as 1250 a fulling mill existed, and St Giles' Mill and Town Mill are often shown on old maps and in older records. By 1539 there were 2 grain-mills and fulling-mills named St Giles' - plus a 'Tanlock' fishery.
The following pieces of information are taken from an article in the Reading Chronicle written by Leslie North, 29 Aug. 1980.

'Millers thus for centuries harnessed the Kennet's flow, and we can be sure they would have been indignant when the proposed canal was suggested in the early part of the 18th century. St Giles' corn mill was

The old mill, Mill Lane

Mill Lane, (showing the Reading Water Works tower in the background) circa 1900

in use until the late 19th century.' and of the Water works:
'Off Mill Lane in 1694 was set up the town's earliest, and exceedingly inefficient, water-supply. An engine in the mill-stream pumped water to a Broad Street reservoir. Power inadequate, these works soon ceased operation. In 1820 a tank-tower 100 ft high and resembling a factory chimney was erected. This served until after 1850, and was not demolished until 1901.

Other Industries

There was a Bacon Factory in Southampton Street. It was called Venners.

Broadbear Brothers, a tin works, was in Katesgrove Lane for a time, until in 1908 increased business meant a move to larger premises in Audley Street. They were in a corner building opposite the tannery.

Eastern Press, a large printers, was in Katesgrove Lane for a number of years in more recent times.

Huntley, Boorne and Steven's, tin works, was on the corner of London Street and Crown Street, extending all the way through to Southhampton Street (at one time). They supplied the biscuit tins to Huntley and Palmers.

Several people recalled Baynes Timber Yard, next to the Jam Factory, in Berkeley Avenue. Slightly further along was Gascoynes, who made milking machinery. They were quite a big employer.

Eric Cooper was an apprentice at a large building in Lynn Street, 'Wheelers', a cabinet makers. It later became Cox's pattern makers. Mr Wheeler had a show room in London Street.

Sid Ballard worked for 15 years for Robert Cort, a large foundry built on the site of Waterloo Kiln. The kiln had moved to Tilehurst. Corts made big valves for gas and water etc., and moved on to make conveyors for coal mines etc. Most of their site has been re-developed as an industrial estate, but Robert Cort still has a presence there.

Les recalled Nicholl's Pickles on the Basingstoke Road, just before the Savoy Cinema, which was on the corner of Buckland Road. This was previously the Voice Cinema.

Chapter Three - Transport

The changes in transport that have occurred over the centuries have had a real effect on all our lives.

In the beginning journeys were made on foot, and then, for a fortunate few, on horseback. This did not change for many centuries. Then came the gradual introduction of the horse and cart, the wagon and horses, and finally coaches and horses. Footways became tracks, and these in turn, became roads. They were very crude to start with, but were gradually improved, and with the invention of Tarmacaddam, they became the roads we know today. Motor vehicles began to appear, and trams were introduced.

 'On Whitley Street, where the roundabout is now, it was known as Whitley Pump. They had trees there and a police box and a hut and seats and these troughs for the horses to go and have a drink out of.

Northumberland Avenue, showing unmade road

Elgar Road (note how wide the road is without cars!)

*A missing link. The shop above at 23 Elgar Road sold its own ginger beer and was owned
by E. Jarrett. The bottle was found by Eric Starmer and dates to late 1800's*

THE OLD PUMP, WHITLEY.

It was also where the tram terminus was. The first tram in the morning was about 5 o'clock, and the last one was at 11 o'clock. On buses and trams years ago if you were on them before 6 o'clock, you could get a workman's ticket, a bit cheaper to go to work.

The wives or sons of the tram people used to bring them tea in a tin can. They used to wait at the top, and when they saw their father on the tram, they used to gave him his tea. The fish shop was the first shop after the houses and the name of that shop was Poulter's. The tram people came up and put their order in so, when they came up on the last tram about quarter to eleven they'd pick up their supper'.

Note: a Turnpike is shown on old maps at the start of the Basingstoke Road, just beyond Whitley Street.

The Railways and Canals

The development of the railway and the canal had great importance for the Reading area and the Katesgrove industries in particular.
W. M. Childs in The Story of the Town of Reading (1905) tells us:

30

By 1810 the town of Reading had gained much from the existence of the canal. It had become an important centre of import and export trade. From the Kennet wharves great quantities of flour, malt, timber, cheese and wool were despatched in barges to London and other markets; while to the same wharves, iron and hardware were brought from Birmingham, stone from Bath, coal from Somerset and Wales, pottery from Staffordshire and groceries from London. Along the roads also came more and more traffic. By day and by night, coaches rattled through the streets.

Much of the larger industry in the area came to depend on the rail system in one form or other. The Co-op Preserve Works had its own railway siding, as did Simond's Brewery and as we have already seen, Waterloo Kiln had its own wharf.

'Coley: Portrait of an Urban Village' (Cusden 1977) tells us:
'From 1909 until the 1970's, the Great Western Railway Central Goods Station was located between Fobney and Willow Streets, (where M & N Cable Laying depot is now) where coal, coke, builders' materials, bananas and other commodities were loaded onto wagons and despatched by a local railway to Southcote where it joined the main-line system at the junction of the West of England and Basingstoke branches'.

The canals and railways had an effect on people's lives but perhaps greater impact was felt by the person in the street when the horse and cart gave way to cars and lorries. Not only did a mode of transport change, but a way of life changed, too. In these hurried days of fast lifestyles and concern about air pollution we can look back to the days gone by and question the changes that were made in the name of progress.

Chapter Four - Home Delivery and Shops

 'There were no cars then. If anybody had a car, and that was in our later years, they were rich. The only traffic you would see on the streets, were carts and barrows. When we moved in 1955 there was only one car in the street. There was only one car for years. You had all your groceries fetched to you. You went to order them, and they came to you on a Tuesday, in a big box. The milkman came to the door, the baker came to the door, they all came to the door'.

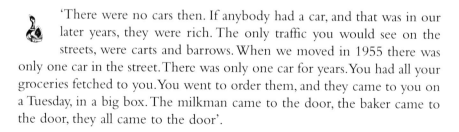 'There were gas lamps in the streets. The copper used to bring the kids in for shinning up them and swinging on the bar at the top'.

'Sid Williams and Bert Peck both had greengrocer rounds, with a horse and cart. You would see Sid at seven in the morning, and he was still up here at ten at night, teeming with rain, with the old oil lamps on the side of the cart. A Mr Ralph used to sell vegetables from a barrow too. Everybody bought their veg from them, you didn't have supermarkets then. They made a living of it, a little living, not rich.

We as kids used to deliver the milk round here. They were just starting to use motorised floats, but when the war came, it was back to horse and cart. The milkmen went off to war, and it was the land army girls who delivered the milk. We helped. If you gave the horse a crust at all, you would suddenly find that during the round, it would wander across and be in your porch waiting for another. On the round you could just take the milk off, the horse just kept going'.

Ann Weight said:

 'The baker used to put the bread through the front window if you weren't in, no one locked their windows then. I used to walk home from school, and would eat the crust.

 'I remember that at 5 o'clock in the afternoon Tibbault's the baker used to come round here (Collis Street) with a horse and cart and

Home delivery

his old bell going ting, ting, ting, and they had these old lamps on the side when it was getting dark, to deliver the bread'.

 'The muffin man came along, and there were people selling bananas on a barrow, 14 for a penny. You had the man with the monkey and the thing, (the organ-grinder).'

 'A chap used to sell winkles on a Sunday. And there was an ice-cream seller, an Italian, (Bercinni) on the corner of Katesgrove Lane'.

 'I remember the fish and chip shop in Elgar Road. There were lots of them in the area, but this one was noted for its faggots and peas. We used to go there with a pudding-basin to collect some; a friend fell off her bike and knocked them flying'.

 'There was a chap called Mr Priest, a colonel type chap who lived in Collis Street opposite Mount Street. He owned two houses together there, and he had windows put in the top so he could observe the stars.'

Pell St, Reading. (1)

'Mr Penny had a shop next door to the fish and chip shop. He had a boathouse at the back, and they used to hire boats out. It was only on a small scale though.'

'The Kennet Arms, on the corner of Elgar Road and Pell Street, had reputedly the coolest drink in Reading, because of the cellar and the dampness from the river. Us kids stood in the bottle and jug, the off-licence part. Nearly every pub had a bottle and jug then'.

'Opposite the Kennet Arms, on Elgar Road, was a Mr King, a builder. He had a yard by the side of his house. You could go and have a bet there, in his front room. It was an unofficial betting shop - you weren't allowed to gamble then. I remember Ellisons, on the corner of Collis Street and Mount Street. It sold general groceries and provisions. It sold ham, cheese, Corona drinks and the first Pepsi Cola. Half way down Collis Street, Mrs Cadell used to sell fruit and vegetables from her front room. This was quite common; there were lots of small shops in the side streets which were ordinary houses with the front room converted into a shop.'

'In Elgar Road I remember a butcher's shop, an electrical shop on the corner of Francis Street, the fish and chip shop which was Macleans. Cooks the bakery was on the other side of the road, where Taylor's betting shop is now, and opposite was Greens, where I used to get 5 cigarettes for Dad. Two doors away from where we lived was Mickle's. It was a grocers, but also used to repair and hire cycles. On the corner of Elgar Road was Eckert's, a sweet shop cum small grocer'.

'Mr Mickle had a yard, next to and behind his shop in Elgar Road, where he used to repair cycles and other things too, such as gramophones, etc. He had collected a lot of bikes in his time, and he used to rent them out for a penny an hour. We kids couldn't afford a bike, and didn't have much money, so we gave him three-happence - enough for an hour and a half. When we used to go and get the bikes, we had packs on our backs, with lunch and a bottle of mineral water in, and we used to go off to Whitley Wood blackberrying or something. We used to come back late, say eight o'clock in the evening. We used to creep up to his yard, sling the bike up against the wall, and run like hell. He knew what was going on.

This shop in Henry Street became 'Mum's Tuck Shop', renowned for its penny drinks and ha'penny chews. Owned by Mrs Griffin at the time

Knott's Brush Factory in Southampton Street

Hale's the butchers in Basingstoke Road

When I grew up, I used to chat to him, and he said "You little beggars (he actually used another word that sounded like beggars), when you used to come back with the bikes, I used to watch you. But at least you used to bring them back.'"

 Wilf Fewtrell recalled Mrs Macteer's shop in Waterloo Road on the corner of Norfolk Street. 'We used to call her 'Mingy Macteer'.

 'There were quite a few shops in Spring Gardens; halfway along was a shop selling fruit and vegetables outside. It also sold toffee apples, and you had to go into the passageway to pay. On the corner where Mount Street met Whitley Street, there used to be a coffee shack (Cecil's). There was an alley that ran between Spring Gardens and Whitley Street, and beyond that was the place you used to take your accumulator (an early battery for radios) for recharging. Next to that was a large mechanical hardware shop called 'Fowler Lees', selling tin baths and scrubbing brushes.'

Whitley Street had more shops than now, and they have changed quite a lot over the years.

'There was an electrical shop run by Mr Ruddle. People used to think he was German, but he was a sergeant in the Home Guard. They used to moan about that'.

Arthur remembers Mr Pottinger's, the hairdressers. His hairdressing equipment is now in the Blake's Lock Museum.

'...during the war, Mr Whitby, who had the camera shop, laid on a film show - Popeye, and what have you, for us kids. He used to show it from his shop, and we could see it in the outside window. There were 20 or 30 of us kids watching it. That sort of thing was new to us. We went to Whitley Hall and paid a penny to see Felix the cat, and that sort of thing. You wouldn't believe it, but we did, and we thoroughly enjoyed it'.

There were lots more pubs in the area than now. There was a pub opposite the Tanyard called the Engineers (remember, the Iron -Works was nearby).

Workers outside the Reindeer Pub (works outing?)

There was a pub on Southampton Street called the Reindeer. Sid Ballard's granny used to own it. 'As a girl she used to have to clean the spittoons, and put down fresh saw-dust. Apparently they used to open at six in the morning, and the men who worked at Simond's brewery used to call in there for a drink before they started work!'

Poverty and the Pawn Shop.

The Pawn Brokers figured in the lives of many people. Indeed, some would argue that the pawn brokers performed a valuable social service. Frank Eyle's Pawn Brokers, at the top of London Street, might sometimes have made a difference as to whether people could afford to eat or not. In general is true to say that people in the Katesgrove area were less well off than we are today.

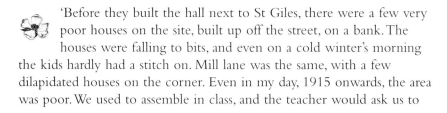
'Before they built the hall next to St Giles, there were a few very poor houses on the site, built up off the street, on a bank. The houses were falling to bits, and even on a cold winter's morning the kids hardly had a stitch on. Mill lane was the same, with a few dilapidated houses on the corner. Even in my day, 1915 onwards, the area was poor. We used to assemble in class, and the teacher would ask us to

put up our hands if we hadn't had breakfast that morning. Whether they had or not I don't know, mind you, but most hands went up and the teacher would send down to Abrahams for halfpenny buns.

We lived in Milman Road. It was a bit more well to do. There were quite a few professional people living in the road. Mind you, we had gas, but no electricity, and for hot water we had to carry water four flights up for a bath. I started work as an office boy in 1923, earning eight bob a week, of which I had to give my mother six. When I got married I was earning the large sum of two pounds and five pence a week. Things were short, and we didn't know what luxuries were, but people were happy then. I remember saying to my first wife one day as I was leaving for work, "Oh lend me sixpence, will you?" She asked me why, and I said that it was to buy a cup of tea and a bun at break time. She said "Do you realise I can get dinner for us for sixpence, steak and kidney pie and potatoes." She was right as well. Things aren't the same now, are they?

Our charlady who worked 2 days a week for half a crown, used to live at the bottom of Silver Street, in one room, with I suppose a toilet at the back. She used to go home from work on a Friday night, and her old chap would give her his money for his week's work, and she would go straight down to the Pawn Shop and get his suit from pawn. He would change into it and would go out drinking, and the suit would go back into pawn again on Monday.'

 'Mum pawned her ring on a Monday, and got it out on Saturday, when Dad got paid.' Eyle's Pawn Brokers continued trading until the 1970's.

Chapter Five - Large Estates

So, hearing accounts of times past and picturing what life was like then we look now at the large estates. The two most notable estates in the area were Whitley Grove and Highgrove.

Whitley Grove

The Whitley Grove estate was a large estate which stretched from the Basingstoke Road just behind Swainstone Road, down to Rose Kiln Lane. From there it followed the Kennet's bank as far as Waterloo Road. Waterloo Kiln was part of the estate.

The following information is taken from the 1886 Sale Catalogue (Reading Library Local Studies Library):

> The estate occupies a conspicuous position on the south side of Reading, about a mile from the centre of this very improving Town, and close to Christ Church, Whitley.

> The Residence is placed on a commanding elevation on the northern side of the property, with fine views many miles in extent across the valley of the Kennet into North Hampshire. The property has considerable attractions as a residential estate, the lawns and gardens being extensive, and the grounds, which are planted with well matured and choice specimen trees, are quite private and well screened both from roads and from adjacent holdings.

> The surface lines of the estate are nicely undulating in character, and there are about twenty acres of valuable brick earth at the point furthest from the residence, and near to the navigable River Kennet.

> The property, which lies in a ring fence, occupies the whole area, between the Basingstoke Road and the River Kennet, to both of which it has very long frontages. There are good roads giving access to the estate on three sides; and the more important frontages were some years ago planted with belts of shrubs, with the view to the development of

the property for Building purposes.

The estate forms part of the favourite suburb of Whitley, which in recent years has largely partaken of the rapid increase of houses and population for which Reading has become conspicuous. The property possesses very marked merits as a building investment. The land near has for years past realised large prices, and considerable areas could be immediately sold off without interfering with the privacy of the residence, while the rents already received shew that the proximity to Reading will always ensure large accommodation rentals. At the northern entrance, on the Basingstoke Road, there is an excellent ornamental Lodge of white brick.

The residence is set well back from the road, from which it is screened by a well-matured plantation, and a winding carriage-way leads to the circular sweep on the eastern side of the residence.

The house is of two storeys and contains on the ground floor: outer lobby, outer hall, inner hall, dining room, 23 ft. by 17 ft., breakfast room, library, small drawing room, 15 ft. by 15 ft., large drawing room, 22 ft. by 17 ft., and WC. On the first floor there are six bedrooms, two dressing rooms, nursery, bathroom and two WC's. Over the kitchens and approached by a second staircase there are three servants' bedrooms. On the north side of the residence there is a large kitchen, 24 ft. by 13 ft., scullery, servants' entrance, china closet, larder, storeroom, butler's pantry and butler's bedroom. The cellarage comprises dairy, two wine cellars and a beer cellar.

At the rear are the usual offices, and coal and wood-houses and yard. In front of the residence is a broad terrace, and from here access is gained to the flower gardens. There is a large expanse of well-kept lawns, interspersed with winding walks, flower beds and rosary. There is a large lawn for lawn-tennis, and below that a croquet ground and a secluded summer house. The large east lawn is surrounded by, and planted with, very rare and well-grown specimen trees. There is also a fernery and aviary, and a conservatory, and a large and excellent kitchen garden.

Highgrove House

There are two stables for six horses, a coach-house for six carriages, a harness room, and a large store-loft for hay. Adjoining the stables is a small enclosed farmery. The park, with nicely scattered timber, extends in front of the residence, south and west, and beyond lies the meadow and arable land, undulating in character, and gradually sloping down to the River Kennet.

The estate was about 122 acres in total, and parts were leased to various people for market-garden purposes, or pasture. As was the intention, parts of the estate were sold off over the years for development. Roads appeared on property that were part of the estate. Hagley Road, Rowley Road, Shenstone Road, and Kinver Road (the original name for the part of the Elgar Road that stretched between Basingstoke Road and Hagley Road) all formed part of one of the building projects. The roads were constructed first and then the houses were built. Gradually the estate shrank in size, and finally the main house was demolished and the remainder developed.

Highgrove

A second substantial estate in the area was Highgrove. This covered an area which stretched from where Highgrove Street is (at the top of Mount Pleasant), right up the east side of Whitley Street where the parade of shops is now, as far as the junction with Christchurch Road, and across to Kendrick Road. It stretched down Kendrick Road until it reached a point opposite the starting point we have indicated, and then the border carried on across to that point. The top corner of Kendrick Road did not belong to the estate, but a sizeable field on the other side of the road did.

The following information is summarised from the sales catalogues held at the local studies library. There was a mansion house with offices which was situated on Whitley Street opposite where Mount Pleasant and Southampton Street join it. Next to that as you went up Whitley Street were stables, a yard and more offices. Then there was an area of extensive kitchen gardens with vineries, a cucumber house and pineries, forcing pits, and orchard houses. This area was set out in an ornamental style, with walks and paths and a fountain, and was screened off from the road by shrubberies with large trees. This garden area stretched right along the edge of Whitley Street, until near the junction where the road curves, where four houses with front and back gardens were.

Just around this corner, where the top end of Highgrove Street is now, was a roadway that led into an area where the Gardener's house and offices was, and also a model farmery. There was a large conservatory and camellia house next to it , and this led down to a fernery, a croquet lawn, shrubberies, a large orchard and paddock. There were paths and walks, a nut walk is mentioned, and a green walk. There were flower beds, and on the edge of the paddock was a lodge.

There was another lodge which was on Kendrick Road, and a wide carriage drive lined with shrubberies and large trees led to the back of the house. On its right was a pinetum, and then there was a path, and then you came to the gardens behind the main house. There was a large lawn, a very formal and ornate Italian Garden, with a central fountain, an American Garden and Border which was less formal, a summer house and rockery, and an aviary or pheasantry. There was also a rosary adjoining the pinetum.

As before, the estate was developed, parcelled into valuable chunks of land and sold to the highest bidder. Highgrove Street was built, and then developed with houses. The area has evolved into what we have today. It is interesting though, to take a few moments to imagine what the two estates were like in their heyday.

Chapter Six - Schools

The schools and Sunday schools in the area have played a very important role in shaping peoples lives.

Katesgrove School

The following information is taken from 'Windows into the Past' - Wynne Frankhum (A resource pack on education in Victorian Britain)
    Education gradually came to be considered more important as Britain

changed from a predominantly rural to a predominantly urban population. There was an increasing need for a literate workforce to work in the new industries created by the Industrial Revolution.

Until the later part of the nineteenth century, education was voluntary and provided mainly by the churches. However, satisfactory mass education could not be provided by voluntary effort, and it became imperative for the Government to become more and more involved in the education of the nation's children.

In 1870 the 'Foster' Education Act passed into law and was instrumental in causing Board schools to be set up. Schools managed by non-denominational School Boards were established, paid for by a local rate. Schools were built and equipped, more and better-paid teachers were employed, the curriculum was widened, and attendance was finally made compulsory in 1880.

The new Board Schools provided a limited education for the working and artisan classes from the age of 5 years to 12, and later, 13 years of age.

Two schools were built to serve the Katesgrove area, in 1873 and 1891, although they occupy the same general site. They succeeded Miss Pell's School, a private infants school, and they were built using the characteristic local brick, like the neighbouring houses. One was built in Gothic style, the other was in a Queen Anne style.

Christchurch School

The following information about Christchurch School was taken from a short booklet written by a previous headmistress G.M. Luxton entitled 'A short account of the work and activities of the school, from its foundation to the present day 1868-1968'.

On July 14th 1868, Christchurch National Schools were opened. Sponsored by the National Society, the schools were built about 5 minutes walk from the Church, in a very quiet part of Reading, on the outskirts of the town. There were approximately 30,000 citizens in the borough in 1868.

Every Monday morning, armed with their School Money, and with pieces of rag to wipe their slates, the children of long ago, set forth. The eldest child of the family paid a penny ha'penny per week, and all the others paid a penny. What a clatter the hob-nailed boots made as the pinafore-clad scholars marched into the school. Very few were late, as a bell, hung high in the roof, was rung.

The Infant's school was in the charge of the Headmistress. Scripture, Reading, Writing, Numbers, Poetry, Marching, and 'Exercises' were taught. The children wrote on slates, the babies being allowed to amuse themselves by 'shredding' pieces of paper. (Children were often sent to school before they were 3 years old.)

Strictly moral poems were taught, and almost daily, the Vicar, Curate, or wealthy people of the Parish, visited the school, and the children sang or read to them.

Discipline was very rigid. In 1878, the Headmistress 'kept the 3rd class in twice this week, for not attending to their Reading lesson'. They were aged 3, 4 and 5. The cane was used very frequently. Children who were slow to learn were dubbed 'Dunces' and demoted.

Frequently in the Winter time, bad weather, Whooping Cough and Measles kept many children away from school, and others, who came without their School Money, were sent home. If the attendance were very poor, one of the Pupil Teachers visited the homes of the absentees. It is recorded that Miss Sarah Orchard, in 1887, on one of her visits, found many children ill with Whooping Cough, Measles and Scarlet Fever. Often the children died of these diseases and also from TB

Infant boys as well as girls were taught sewing, and we read that, in 1884, the boys 'commenced hemming handkerchiefs for the examination'.

The Infants' School, 180 strong in 1892, was ill-lit, inadequately warmed. The rooms were overcrowded and there was insufficient lavatory accommodation, yet, 'The children are very bright and happy, and their Instruction is excellent, both in manner and method', says Her Majesty's Inspector.

Excellent progress is recorded too, in the Boys' and Girls' Schools. Scripture, writing, arithmetic, reading, grammar, geography and singing were taught.

Good manners and 'tone' were taught also. Miss Luxton was surprised to find that when she mounted the stage for the first time in 1950, that when she greeted the children, the girls curtsied to her and the boys saluted. A delightful touch of Old England, she remarked.

Lateness and idleness were not tolerated, and strict honesty was taught.

It was not all hard work and seriousness though. There is a record which tells of the joy given each August, by the School Feast. This treat was held in a nearby field, and the school was closed on that day. Often, apparently, at this time of year, girls stayed away to go to the fair.
In 1869, Mr Wilson paid for the whole school to see Wombwell's Menagerie. Both Mr Wilson, and Mr Attenborough, (of Whitley Grove), gave the school several 'treats in their grounds'.

There is also an account of the terrific excitement, when one Saturday, an outing to Binfield took place. Mr Jarvis supplied a wagonette and two horses, and on payment of two shillings and five and a half pence per child, a delighted crowd of girls set off for a day's enjoyment in the country.

In 1911, swimming was introduced, and a weekly visit to King's Meadows Baths took place during the summer, the girls walking both ways. Parents were also asked to provide 'pumps' for Drill. Physical Education was beginning to come into its own.

Coley swimming bath, used by many local school children

George Palmer School

This was the third school in the area, and it too, was instrumental in providing a good education for its many pupils over the years. Part of it later became Cintra secondary school.

The British School

Opened in 1811 the British School was one of Reading's earliest free schools. Although it was originally housed elsewhere the British School moved to a building on Southampton Street. At the time of writing this the building is under threat of re-development.

The British School was based on a system of education invented by Mr Joseph Lancaster, a Quaker. It was a charitable institution for poor boys and was well in advance of its time. As a Quaker, Lancaster was opposed to physical punishment involving pain but not opposed to discipline. Lancaster used shackles and cages in which offenders were hung from the rafters. This was designed to disgrace the perpetrator and encourage shame. The 'cage' was a tradition. It was said to have hung in the main hall long after disuse.

Lancaster stated that pupils were taught reading, writing, and arithmetic 'to render them more useful members of society, without any reference whatsoever to sect or party in religious opinions.' For writing exercises there were flat desks covered with a thin layer of sand! Sheets were taken from a spelling book and placed before each class and pointed to, until every word was recognised and spelt. Passages from the bible were treated in a similar way.

The school was very successful and was expanded to take girls and infants. It eventually closed in 1902 having provided a decent education for the poor of Katesgrove for many years.

Taken from 'A History of Education in Reading' by LW Harman.

The Tank

The Tank, or Spring Gardens Recreation Ground, as it used to be known, is situated close to Whitley Street. The back gardens of the houses on the west side bordering one edge and the back gardens of the houses on the north side of Essex Street bordering another edge.

It is used today as a play area, but previously was a proper recreation ground, with its own keeper. There were several keepers, one of which was a Mr Dungey, who was the Father-in-law of Felix Bowness, the television personality. If you search it out today, you may well wonder what its history is. It is quite an uncommon feature. We wondered too. Edna and Les Plested thought that the tank was a swimming pool at one time. They remembered Les's mum swimming in it. They also remembered that when it was a recreation ground the keepers house was right by the entrance. Les learnt to ride his bike at the tank.

Old maps of the area tell us that the tank had been a reservoir for the local waterworks company. One end of Spring Gardens was formerly known as Tank Road. It has not been a reservoir for many years, much to the benefit of local children, who have enjoyed many hours of play there.

Chapter Seven – The Meadows the Way they Were

Waterloo Meadows is the site which is bordered by the River Kennet, Elgar Road South, and Rose Kiln Lane. The Reading Evening Post in October 1980 reported that: For many years the Katesgrove Residents Association has been campaigning to have the land turned into a public park.

The major obstacle at the time was that half the land belonged to Berkshire County Council, but this was resolved when the Borough Council bought it for the then princely sum of seventeen thousand pounds. This meant that plans drawn up by the Reading Waterways Group and the Waterways Trust could be implemented, and with the help of the Council's recreation department, work started in earnest to transform the site from an area of rough land left after the landfill operation, to something like the meadows we know today. Had the borough council and the residents association not worked together in this way, Waterloo Meadows as we know it today might be very different.

The Katesgrove Clarion, which was the newsletter for the Katesgrove Residents Association, reported in September 1981: This summer, volunteers started work in the meadows clearing the way for the creation of Reading's Kennetside park. In November 1982 it reported: a tree planting campaign, the planting of thousands of saplings in three copses named after local streets (Elgar, Alpine and Milman), the building of a footbridge, with the help of the Army apprentices from Arborfield, and a planned all-weather path across the Meadows. Many trees have also been planted in memory of local people. In May 1983, work was started on a new play structure, and the distinctive Children's Centre was opened in 1989 by T.V. personality Floella Benjamin.

The writers, researchers and editors who compiled Waterloo Sunrise were brought together by a group called 'The Friends of Waterloo Meadows' hereafter referred to as 'The Friends' or FOWM. The group was formed in 1993 by Tim Hall who was chair of the group from 1993 to 1998 to look after Waterloo Meadows. In addition to this, the group has an interest in the wedge of green land which is the Kennet Meadows which extends past

Local residents planting a tree in
Waterloo Meadows

Southcote and towards the M4. Local people have many historical recollections of Waterloo Meadows and these are included here in what has become a focal point for this book and for people's recollections of the area.

When people of the older generation say 'This was all fields when I was young' it sounds like a bit of a cliché but this is true for much of Reading. The following accounts tell us of Waterloo Meadows and the surrounding area, and what the area meant to people, many of whom have lived in the area all their lives.

Play structure at Waterloo Meadows

Waterloo Meadows Children's Centre nearing completion

Mr Paintin was born on 6th January 1918 in Elgar Road. At the time of writing he still lives there. His recollections tell us of a completely different childhood than would be described today.

 'Elgar Road was backed by what we called the 'kiln'. This was not correct; it was the worked out clay pit that had supplied a kiln that was at the junctions of Francis Street, Alpine Street and Elgar Road. In those days much of the slopes were bare of any growth and were still settling. After heavy rain the clay was always on the move and could be dangerous. Eventually grass, bushes, trees (including apple trees) covered most of the slopes; all gone now - four blocks of flats instead!

Gone are the butterflies, first red admirals and small tortoiseshells, an occasional deep yellow brimstone and large white, but midsummer, clouds of small whites, a few blues - hard to see, but they were there, then small browns. There were frogs at one time. Foxes visited mostly at night and a few hedgehogs. There were plenty of birds, mostly sparrows and the blackbird with its beautiful song. Later on there were starlings. A hawk would hover. Wasps nested in the cracks in the clay and were to be avoided. One day in each year the ants would fly, settling everywhere and discarding their wings, then scuttling about.

There was also a sand pit, a pocket of clean sand where the youngest played; nearly all homes had several children. We were seldom on the streets unless it was too wet at the back, and then not after dark. Rainy days were spent reading, writing, or drawing, and I suspect squabbling with my sister.

As we got older we could take part in other activities: - digging trenches over the Kiln, playing at soldiers - us v the Germans naturally. This involved throwing clumps of clay at each other, but I don't recall much harm being done. We used to make a fire in an old tin with a wire handle attached so one could swing it around the head to keep it going. Sometimes the tin became disconnected and the fire would go sailing away.

Another game we played was 'Urky, Urky', a form of hide and seek. A few stones were put in a tin, the end stamped shut to make a rattle. Someone was selected (or bullied) into staying at base whilst the rest of us hid while he counted up to a hundred or whatever. The object was then to stay hidden, at the same time trying to get back to base; if seen the baseman rattled his tin, shouting 'Urky, Urky' and calling out the name. This game didn't last long, it usually ended up with squabbling.

The girls were kept under strict control and most helped their mothers,

The 'kiln'

Work in progress to shore up the 'kiln/banks'
Some of the houses were in danger of falling off!

The shoring up work finished - the Tippett Rise flats under construction

otherwise they had their dolls and skipped a lot. Spinning tops had their days, hoops (wooden mostly - steel for the elite). We played 'leap frog' or 'puff coming' in the street. Football was played on the way home from school - the lamp posts were on the edge of the pavement, between them and the fence was the goal.

On snowy days we took a home-made sled over the kiln, but it had no good 'runs' so we walked up to Prospect Park to use the slopes there. When the farm was disused we used to play football over the meadows. For a time Elgar Rovers Football club used a paddock at the far end for training.

The R100 and Waterloo Meadows

Sid Ballard can remember seeing the R100 over the meadows. This would have been the Concorde of its day.

 'The R100 caused quite a stir when it made an appearance over the Meadows. One day it came over and it hovered over the fields quite a while. Evidently, they dragged ropes down, and they tried to land it in the meadows, but whether there was some fault with it, I don't know, but it cleared off.'

The R100 was an airship, and a sister ship to the R101, which crashed in 1930, killing 46 people. The Daily Mail reported on the 6 October 1930:

> The terrible news that R101, the largest and finest airship yet constructed, had been destroyed in France in the first stage of her voyage to India with 46 of the 54 persons on board her, including the British Air Secretary, Lord Thomson, came as a shock to the nation today.

> Her departure from Cardington on Saturday night was dramatic. One of the engines was sluggish. Ballast had to be thrown out to make her rise. She travelled very slowly to the coast, and many people thought that she was ominously low. Over France she encountered a fierce storm. Then came the disaster.

> Survivors state that apparently something had gone wrong with the steering gear, after which they believe that a gas escape was created (possibly by the airship hitting the ground or trees when no longer under proper control). There was an explosion and the ship burst into flames.

Among those who perished in R101 are almost all the British experts in the art of airship design. The Air Ministry promised a full public enquiry.

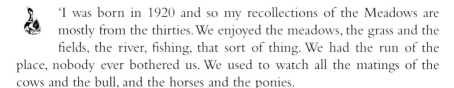 'I was born in 1920 and so my recollections of the Meadows are mostly from the thirties. We enjoyed the meadows, the grass and the fields, the river, fishing, that sort of thing. We had the run of the place, nobody ever bothered us. We used to watch all the matings of the cows and the bull, and the horses and the ponies.

From time to time, they used to have the Scouts from Reading down here, at St. Michael's church, and they used to go camping in the meadows, by the side of the river. Us lads nearly all had a boat of some sort, and we joined in with a big punt. We used to go off of an evening, or in the summer we'd get our punts and go to the place called Monkey Island, which is further up the river, beyond the pumping station. We'd have a good splash about, and what not.

From time to time we used to make our own boats. But what happened mostly was, that people who lived by the river used to push up on the bank any old boat they wanted to get rid of. Us kids would patch them up and use them.

Another thing we used to do when we were a bit older, was to gamble in a small way. There was a black shed (the black barn?), by the side of the river which had a ditch about 3 or 4 feet wide running along in front of it. We used to take the plank away and gamble in the shed. At the back of it, onto the river, were sheets of corrugated iron. We'd work it loose so we had an escape route. We had a "Skib" or boy, keeping watch, and when the policeman came and was trying to get across the ditch, we were through the back, into our boats, and up the river.

We never gambled a lot, only pennies, cards and things. We were trespassing, but we never did any damage. We used to play cards for pennies, and whoever was keeping "skibo", used to get a halfpenny a game. So he made about sixpence.

Mr Bucknell used to let the fair use the meadows twice a year. It was a big fair.

When the farm finished, the council tipped on the meadows to build the land up. It used to flood regularly. The houses on the river side of Elgar Road, the water used to come right up their back gardens, and would flood their sculleries, so they could not use them. I remember one lady who used to live opposite the bottom of Alpine Street. My wife and I went to see her, and there was a mark on the wall where the water came up to. So they altered all the locks, and they built the meadows up, and it does not flood now.

I remember St. Michael's church well, it was a lovely little church. I was a choir-boy, cub scout and boy scout there. By the area where we used to play football, was a ditch, where all the water that drained off the banks used to go to, and we kids used to play in it. We had a right old time!

We didn't have time to get into too much mischief, though, – there was too much going on, always something of interest. We used to go across to the brick-kiln and watch them, we helped the farmer, we played football on the area behind Elgar Road.'

St Michael's Church. This building later became the Glossifilm factory

'The Meadows' was where most of the kids learnt to swim. As you came across from Waterloo Road they had cleared it - well, dredged it, the bigger lads from Elgar Road; and that area was the place where nearly everyone learnt to swim. There was a flat bit just past the barn where some of them had punts, so we went to swim in that area. There was a ditch at the back of the semis, which had water in it and we used to jump it. On the other side of the river there was a place where the jam factory let the warm water out, and the fish used to congregate there. We all used to fish there.

We used to call the meadows the hayfields. There was a second field in the hayfields. They used to be able to put a bar across, and where they put special cows who were in calf. There were woods at the back of the semis.

When I was a kid, as you went down Waterloo Road, on the left were allotments and pig-sties. Quite a few people kept pigs there. I used to help clean the pigs out ..... my mum used to go potty! The chap that owned the greengrocers behind the coffee-stall on Whitley Street, Sid Williams, had pigs there. So did a chap called Bailey, and another chap, Hughes.

Most people kept chickens in their back gardens, you had one for Christmas; there weren't supermarkets then. We lived in Waterloo Road, 5 girls, 3 boys, Mum, Dad, my sister's chap. We only had 2 bedrooms! We were a very happy family. We used to help all around. My Mum used to give all the kids bread and dripping. During the war you were allowed cake and things, as well as biscuits if you worked at Huntley and Palmers. I had 3 sisters there, a brother and a brother in law. They called them together at one time, and wanted to know what they did with the stuff they took home - there was enough to feed an army! We used to give it away to people that lived near us.

The land behind Elgar Road (where Tippett Rise flats are now), was flat and the men from Elgar Road used to play football on it. The Tug of War teams used to practice there, in preparation for the fetes.

There were quicksands at the bottom of the banks. One of my friends got caught in one. Luckily we pulled him out with a mudguard. He'd lost his wellingtons in it. I didn't dare tell my mum.

We used to play on the banks during our holidays. Our Mum would go to Woolworth's and buy for me and my elder brother 2 pairs of khaki shorts and 2 khaki shirts. They used to last us our 6 weeks holiday, one on, one off.

Our Mum used to hate bonfires, and would smell us as we came in. 'Have you been having bonfires?' Oh no, not us! We used to nick spuds from the allotments and bake them around a fire.'

 'The meadows led to the 'ballisoles' (ballast holes) which were further up the river. Men went there, betting, playing cards, gambling, swimming, anything.

Ann Weight was born in Collis Street in 1943. She recalls what the meadows were like in her early years.

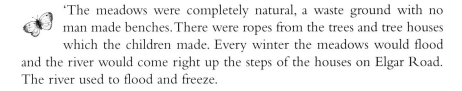 'The meadows were completely natural, a waste ground with no man made benches. There were ropes from the trees and tree houses which the children made. Every winter the meadows would flood and the river would come right up the steps of the houses on Elgar Road. The river used to flood and freeze.

The meadows then were more of a wooded copse with a path running through and old gnarled trees that the boys used to climb. There was an open area in the meadows where the fair used to come. There were swinging boats and chairoplanes, a helter-skelter, shooting ranges, hook the duck and roll a penny. There were coconut shies with big chalk dogs as prizes. I wasn't supposed to go to the fair because I was too young. However, I once sneaked off to the fair alone. When I returned home I found mother out looking for me! That was the only time she ever hit me.'

David Geary was Mayor from 1994 - 1995. He and Percy Thatcher worked together at the CO-OP printing works and from their work place they could see the meadows. They witnessed some of the changes that occurred in the meadows in the 50's and 60's.

 'I always used to like the way the meadows kept you in touch with the seasons. You'd notice when all the trees came into leaf and then when all the may blossom was on the trees. Every morning before we started work we'd go out and have a look. My office overlooked the meadows. There were beautiful, beautiful sunsets there in the evenings. I remember the electric pylons going up. That was horrific. It changed them. Then you had the relief road. The relief road and the pylons; they changed them for us.'

 'Rose Kiln Lane shook me. They seemed to finish that in no time once they'd started. We never thought that area would be anything in our time. When it was a landfill site we watched it all being filled up. It started about 1950.

Halcyon Days - Mike Cox

Mike Cox is Chair of Friends Of Waterloo Meadows at the time of going to press. He recalls his childhood living in the Katesgrove area.

'At the time, Oh, what heady days they were! They stretched before us and seemed to have no limit.

These were the days of summer in my youth, and I guess it is the same for every generation. You had no responsibilities. Your parents worked hard to put food in your belly and clothes on your back. Life was for living, and we made sure we lived it to the full. It consisted of endless days, friends to play with, brilliant places to play, (this certainly makes a difference), super-heroes and sweets. What more could you want?

In the early 60's I was between ten and twelve. We played in many different places. I suppose being a boy, this was easier for me; also, our parents trusted us to look after ourselves. And I suppose, they thought we would be safe; not the case now.

We played in the Tank, (this was the large empty reservoir just off Whitley

Street). The play equipment they had in there seemed really massive to us. I particularly remember the large "swingboat". It consisted of a long swinging seat, not unlike a scaffold plank, with things to hold on to, and this was slung beneath two supporting frames, one near either end. You swung it like a swing, and the brave ones amongst us, would take it right up to the limit of its swing. It was quite fearsome to me.

I remember too, that we used to run up the almost vertical walls of the tank, to retrieve footballs or cricket balls which would invariably escape when we played games.

The other good thing about the Tank, apart from it being a great place to play, was that Mr Miller's store was right by it. What brilliant sweets and drinks we could get then! Jamboree Bags, Lucky Bags, Flying Saucers, Shrimps, Love Hearts, Blackjacks, Penny Chews, washed down with Tizer or Vimto. A favourite of mine were Jubblies, which was like a huge iced pop which was a strange shape, a bit like a pyramid. They went on and on, bliss!

We played over the kiln, or over the banks. This was the rough ground, and old workings of the clay-pits that were between Elgar Road and the roads on top of the hill, Edgehill, Waldeck, Collis, Milman, etc. We made camps, we had battles. Clay-wanging was a favourite. There was lots of clay exposed in places, and you attached a ball of it to the end of a willow stick, and holding it behind your head, you "wanged" it.

You brought it forward with some force so that the clay ball came flying off and went hurtling towards your opponent. By doing this you could throw a lump of clay with some force, over a considerable distance, with great accuracy, and could inflict a stinging, bruising wound on your enemy. Great fun!

Another favourite was to slide down the hillside on whatever you could lay your hands on. Trays, fridge-doors, whatever. There was a really good slide below the end of Edgehill Street, I think. It was about 25 yards long I suppose, quite steep, and apart from being the exposed hillside, there was also ash on it, and sometimes rubbish. This was brilliant though, and as you neared the bottom at some speed, there was a bump in the ground and you effectively became airborne for a second, before coming down in a bit of a hollow at the bottom. We had a large piece of corrugated iron, which was turned up at the front, like a sledge, and 5 or 6 of us could sit on this and would hurtle down. This we named the 'Tokyo Express'.

We would spend a lot of time over the kiln. We would play football on the flat part at the bottom, we would stick bangers into the clay and light them; we even took our first tentative steps towards smoking. I wont go into what we did, but it was probably worse for your health than smoking proper. It was a great playground for us, although we did stay away from some areas where there were supposedly quicksands.

We also played over the hayfields, where Waterloo Meadows is now. It hadn't been that long since it was a tip. There were quite a few areas where strange blue patches were on the surface, where nothing would grow. We played up the allotment end, and had great fun playing a game in the long grass. We crawled along and made alleys in the grass as we went, and played a game that was a cross between chase and hide 'n' seek By the time we had finished it looked like someone had made a maze in the grass. Looking back, I don't know who this area of grass belonged to, but it seemed to be a hay-cutting area, rather than just rough grass. I bet they cursed us.'

Chapter Eight - War Time

The shock waves of the war were felt all over England and meant different things to different people. Some people we talked to could remember elements of the first world war. Mr Cooper remembers a Mr Potts whose picture was in the local school. Mr Potts won the Victoria Cross for bravery at Gallipoli.

The Roll of Honour states:
> Trooper Frederick William Owen Potts
> For most conspicuous bravery and devotion to a wounded comrade in the Gallipoli Peninsula. Although himself severely wounded in the thigh in the attack on Hill 70 on August 21st, 1915, he remained out

over 48 hours under the Turkish trenches with a private of his regiment who was severely wounded and unable to move, although he could himself have returned to safety. Finally, he fixed a shovel to the equipment of his wounded comrade, and, using this as a sledge, he dragged him back over 600 yards to our lines, although fired on by Turks on the way. He reached our trenches at about 9.30 p.m. on the 23rd.

Trooper Potts served in the Berkshire Yeomanry, and was the first Yeoman to win a VC. He was also the first Reading man to gain one, and the honour brought to Berkshire by one of her sons was commemorated by handsome presentations.

Berkshire in the War, Reading Standard Pictorial Record, wrote of him in 1916:

> The Mayor, aldermen and burgesses of Reading offered an illuminated address of civic congratulation, the scroll being contained in a silver casket. Trooper Potts accepted the gifts proudly but modestly.

After the war he resumed his career as a tailor, in Edgehill Street, and stood as an anti-socialist candidate for Katesgrove in a council election. His death was announced in November 1943, he died in a nursing home, aged 50.

 'I used to walk to work, passing the Labour Exchange in London Street, seeing those poor ex-servicemen queuing up outside for the 14 bob a week benefit. Some of them didn't have a decent overcoat on cold, bitter mornings, and were pale and gaunt, and obviously hungry. Silver Street was rough; I can remember standing watching with my mouth wide open.'

Many of our contributors remember the Katesgrove area during the Second World War and the changes it brought to the area.

'I have very good memories of the meadows during the Second World War. The meadows were where we played and swam. We had a big black barn which we used as a changing place. There was a big

Troops in Southampton Street

willow tree by the river beside the barn. We made a big swing and we could swing out and let ourselves into the river. We also made a diving board. Great fun!

There was the farm cottage and big orchard where Mr and Mrs Coyle and family lived. During the summer, families would come to the meadows to picnic and fish and swim. It was a very good area for birds and wildlife. The meadows in summer were full of sky larks. After we had been swimming we used to go into Mr Eckert's shop, opposite, at the bottom of Waterloo Road and Elgar Road. Mr Eckert was a naturalised German. He was very good for sweets if you had used all your coupons; he always seemed to be able to let you have some.

During the war the American soldiers would come from the CO-OP builing across the meadows fishing, swimming, and sunbathing. Then the German and Italian prisoners of war came to the meadows, clearing and dredging the river. We had fun using their boats and rafts. When there was an air raid we felt safer in the meadows than in the air raid shelters.

At the end of the war a small firm called Beardmore and Co. made breeze

A military funeral in Southampton Street

blocks and concrete blocks at the entrance to the meadows. After the war Traylens fair used the meadows. To bring it up to date now I think this must be the only free fishing in Berkshire. I think FOWM have done a very good job preserving the meadows. If they had not done so I think it would have been more factories and roads.' (However, we digress.)

'I remember the meadows from 1937 when I was about 9. I went to Christchurch School and I left there in 1939 to go to Katesgrove school. I had just started and after about a week I remember the headmaster calling us all together to say that our friend Hitler had sent us on a holiday, because all the evacuees were coming to Reading.

Double-decker buses began to arrive at Christchurch school, people getting off, all the kids getting off with their labels on their lapels, people going up, if they wanted to, to try to pick the people they wanted in their house. They might have known the people, or if they were going to take a family with two kids say.

They came from London, from the Kennington area, the Oval, Lambeth - we called them "the Laandeners".

A local VE Day celebration

Each evacuee was given a big packet of sweets. I remember a whacking great bar of Cadbury's chocolate. We sat down over "the banks" with these kids and we ate chocolate, chocolate, chocolate!

I remember a big house in Milman Road called Highclere. It was where all the kiddies before the war that didn't have mums and dads, or they were separated lived. We called them the home children. They were always prim and proper, because they were dressed by the home.'

'I remember that there were Italian prisoners of war on the meadows during the war. They worked on the farm. A Dane was in charge of them. I think they went back to a camp in the evening. One of them made me a belt from sweet papers. It was really pretty.'

'The evacuees from London thought the allotments in Arkwright Road were growing wild and helped themselves to our fruit and vegetables. I was glad when they went back to London.'

Land Army girl cutting kale

Chapter Nine – The Farm at Waterloo Meadows

Local people recall the life of the meadows when it was largely used for farming.

The Farm in Mr Wiggins' time

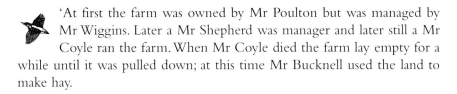

'At first the farm was owned by Mr Poulton but was managed by Mr Wiggins. Later a Mr Shepherd was manager and later still a Mr Coyle ran the farm. When Mr Coyle died the farm lay empty for a while until it was pulled down; at this time Mr Bucknell used the land to make hay.

Mr Wiggins was farm manager in the early 1920's. Mr Wiggins had a wife, but no children and he ran the farm with one man. This extended from 198, Elgar Road to Basingstoke Road, to (now called) Cradock Road to the River Kennet. The piece – now Waterloo Meadows, was flooded most of January/February. There was grass for about 20 cows or hay in turn. Another field on the north side of Elgar Road up as far as Collis Street was ploughed each year and planted with marigolds or kale (we called it cow cabbage). None of the rest of the land had the plough to it.'

'Mr Wiggins used to wear a hat on his head like a half coconut when he was milking.'

'If Mum found herself in need of extra milk we could take a jug to the farmhouse for what we needed although the milkman called each day.'

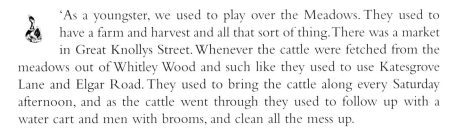

'As a youngster, we used to play over the Meadows. They used to have a farm and harvest and all that sort of thing. There was a market in Great Knollys Street. Whenever the cattle were fetched from the meadows out of Whitley Wood and such like they used to use Katesgrove Lane and Elgar Road. They used to bring the cattle along every Saturday afternoon, and as the cattle went through they used to follow up with a water cart and men with brooms, and clean all the mess up.

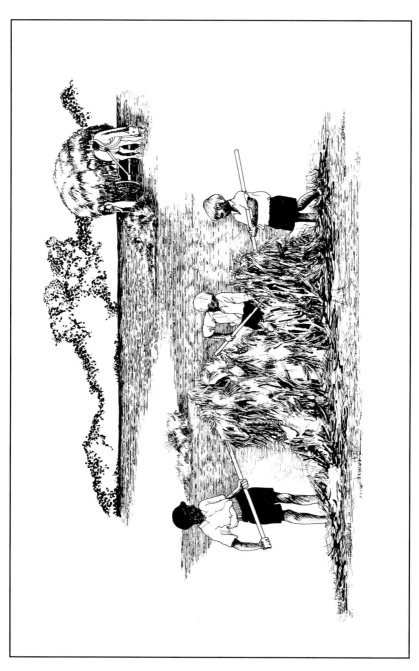

Children helping with hay making

As a boy I'd help drive the cattle to market with Mr Wiggins. It was a large farm with pigs, cattle and livestock such as chickens, geese and ducks. During the bad weather the doors of the barn were left open and the cattle sheltered there. The farmers would go to the gate and call the cattle in and they would all come to their own positions in the milking shed. We used to go down there and learn how to milk. All the cows had names like Dolly and Daisy etc. We didn't milk as well as the farmers but every little helped. The milk from the farm was put through coolers. The milk was also sent to dairies, I presume. They had churns.

We also used to go to the farm to collect milk, eggs and butter, all fresh.

When you walked through the farm there were barns and cattle sheds, and above the top of them they used to keep all the cattle food. Just in front of them was a big round thing with a belt on that went to the top. What actually happened was that they attached a horse who kept going round and round, and the "splat" went round and it chewed up all the cow cake and that. We used to watch all the matings of the cows and the bull, and the horses and the ponies.

At haymaking we used to watch and sometimes help. You went round with a horse with a grass-cutter, and then you went round with a reaper, piled it into lines, and when it was dry, you collected it up and put it onto a haystack. There were perhaps three or four haystacks.'

Mr Sheppard's time

 'It was later when Mr Sheppard took over the farm and was for many years the manager. Happy days were spent helping with the hay making, and we were able to gather the hay and build the ricks. As we finished our job we were given lemonade and ice-cream; what wonderful days!

I remember that there were four meadows, and they used to grow cow-kale, turnips, cabbages corn and such like in them from time to time, all to feed the cattle. In Mr Shepherd's time, behind Collis Street there was a line of trees - we used to call them the "millionaires".'

This creates an impressive image of tall trees standing behind Collis Street, looking stately as they watched over the valley. However, as we have already heard, parts of the Whitley Grove estate were secluded by the planting of large specimen trees and so the term millionaires might refer to the people behind the trees rather than the trees themselves.

 'Horses were running loose in the Meadows. Yeomanry House in Castle Street was a Territorial Army place, and they had horses. The horses were kept in the Meadows, and we kids used to ride them. Twice a week, my brother was one of them, they used to take the horses from the Meadows, take them for training, and then bring them back.'

The time of The Coyle family and Mr Bucknell

 'The farm was eventually taken over by Mr Bucknell from Southcote farm and he only used it for grazing his cattle. He hired the Meadows for his dry but in-calf cows. When the calves were born in the field his men would fetch the calf in a cart - the cow walking behind - to Southcote. Later on Mr Bucknell modernised the dairy operation and a truck used to pick the milk up and take it to Coley.'

Dave Ballard adds:

 'The house opposite the farm was also owned by Mr Bucknell. The chap living there was a Mr Vockins; he was a bailiff, I think. He used to keep hay and goats in the black barn. We used to let the goats out, and he used to chase us. He had a really big Billy-goat, and we really had to move when it chased us. The goat kids with their little stumps of horns were great fun, but if they caught you they really packed a punch when they butted you.

There was also a bull in the fields. It had a mask on. We used to remove the mask and it would run amok. It ended up in the garden of the semis, one time.'

'The Coyle Family lived in the farm house. We used to call it the cottage, and when you went in there you walked on stone. It was all flagstones from front to back. There were three children, son Geoffrey, daughter Peggy and another son called John. John was what you would now call Down's Syndrome.

I used to play with Peggy and Geoffrey. It was a big farmhouse with a very big garden, with vegetables, apple trees and an outside loo. I don't know if someone decided to pull the cottage down, but Mrs. Coyle lost her husband and they moved soon afterwards'.

This marked the end of an era for Waterloo Meadows. There had been a farm shown on the meadows since the Tithe map of 1841 and before that. The days when the locals could pop to the farm for extra milk, take part in the haymaking and the milking were long gone. Soon to be gone also, was the ability to walk the cows to market, along Elgar Road, down Katesgrove Lane and into Great Knollys Street. The farmers had cared for the land; it was closely tied to their well-being and their livelihoods. Now the meadows must have new custodians if they are to survive the ravages and demands of modern life and to exist for our children to enjoy.

Chapter Ten - The Landfill Site at Waterloo Meadows

'Elgar Road always used to be under water until in the 1950's they started filling the fields. There was no Rose Kiln Lane, only a wooden bridge for walking over the river which was made wider for cars. The bridge was slatted so you could see the water running underneath. The meadows were very different. I remember a great big hole, the height of this house. All the rubbish was pushed over the edge but now the meadows are all flat. The filling was all planned. It was done in sections: fill, cover, next section, fill, cover etc. By the gate (approx. 198 Elgar Road) there was a hut for the workmen at the tip. Sundays were overtime and I used to ride down to check everything was OK. I would ride down with my daughter Rita, or one of her brothers.

There were lots of seagulls flying around and rooks, starlings and sparrows.

It was very messy in winter, especially in high winds. I used to drive a bulldozer. It got very cold in winter especially if you worked at the top where you needed to wear lots of coats.

The meadows were filled by the mid 1950's. I worked down Elgar Road for 4 years or more. It used to smell dreadful at the tip. People would walk down the road holding their noses. Big beds of sewage and sludge were dumped at the tip. At the end of each day a man went round spraying with powder, to keep the smell down I think.

Children from Elgar Road used to play on the tip. The landfill was gradually filled in as we went along. Behind the part we were working on at the time grass would grow up and the kids would make camps out of the rubbish. There were a lot of rats on the tip. They used to kill the rats with ferrets and used the ferrets to kill the rabbits, too, for food. I had two ferrets for a while. When I was a kid people could live on the stuff they grew and on the rabbits they caught. Nothing was wasted in those days, especially in wartime.

Household rubbish went into the landfill. We used to save bottles and the papers because you got money on them. Different coloured glass was put in different bins. When they were full they were taken away and broken up. We used to keep paper, cardboard, clothes and bicycles. The bikes would be pinched by kids to do up. There were always kids hanging around the tip. Once a month we would get a bonus based on the stuff we had saved.

Reading Corporation kept pigs. We saved peelings etc. to be collected for the pigs. Fruit, vegetables and other out of date stuff was sent to the landfill by shops and would be kept for the pigs. There were pig sties at the back of the allotments. People kept pigs at their allotments and had to buy waste food and scraps from the Corporation.'

Rita Brown is William Newport's daughter. She recalls:
'My father would bring loads of stuff home from the tip. Mum made him put it in the shed. I used to have penny sales from the stuff in the shed and I used to have a nice time in the shed looking round'.

74

The path into Waterloo Meadows

Waterloo Meadows looking towards St. Giles's Church

Chapter Eleven – A Year in the Life of Waterloo Meadows

The final section of this book belongs to Waterloo Meadows itself and it is fitting that the area that brought the editors and researchers of this book together should have the last word. So often in this world we take what is there for granted. In terms of species we may worry about what we have already lost, or have no power over, instead of celebrating and conserving what we have now. It was for this reason that the Katesgrove Community book project chose to document as much about Waterloo Meadows as possible, not only in terms of personal histories but in terms of the wildlife – the flora and fauna.

This section of the book gives a month by month account of the change in the meadows through the seasons and I hope we will create for you a picture of this open space that lies between the terraces of Elgar Rd, the industrial estate of the A33 and the heavy traffic of Rose Kiln Lane. Bordered by the River Kennet, the wildlife is rich and varied and we hope it will be captured for present and future generations.

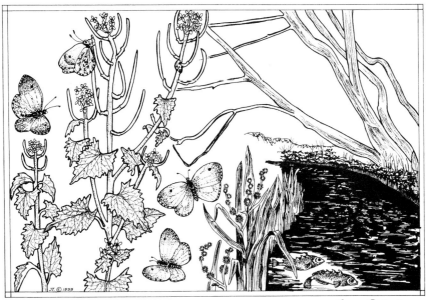

end of May

End of May 1996

The path from Makro to the river is flanked by hedge garlic. This is accompanied by the orange tip butterfly, it being food for the larvae. As we moved along the path to clear the way from brambles and stinging nettles we were greeted by a flutter of these tiny marmalade clad butterflies.

A fire last year had razed a large patch to the ground to the left of the path just before you reach the allotment fence, only to be reclaimed by crisp white hoary cress and patrolled by a lone pair of May flies. White bladder campion lines the path and contrasts with the two varieties of comfrey.

On this occasion the stream is in good condition and the sticklebacks swim happily in the bubbling shallows. The stream is flanked by cracked willows and a FOWM created shallow, now boasts water mint , brooklime, branched bur-reed, meadowsweet, hemlock water dropwort and amphibious bistort. Vetch hides amongst the tall grasses along with the dead nettle.
The May blossom is officially late this year due to the cold Spring. The black thorn is four weeks late and the May (hawthorn) comes usually two weeks later (television programme Country File). The old expression "Ne'er cast a clout till May is out" certainly holds true this year as the May blossom did not venture out until the ambient temperatures raised. Until then it had remained firmly shut.

As you walk towards Rose Kiln Lane from the Children's centre the meadow is submerged under a sea of cow parsley. The elder is just beginning to flower, a sure sign that things <u>are</u> late this year.

The heron has visited the site several times early this spring and has rewarded our vigilant early rising members with spectacular views. Similarly, the elusive king fisher has fished at top speed, flying fast and low as it begins its breeding season.

The patches of wildflowers sown by FOWM are just beginning to flower. The horse chestnut blossom is beginning to form. A carpet of white poplar blossom lines the path to the meadow from the children's centre and the fruits of the field maple hang like small moths. As I leave the path for home I notice the tarmac drive is flanked by pineapple mayweed.

end of June

End of June

By now the hawthorn blossom on the trees that line the drive way is nearly over and even at this stage in the summer the crab apples on the apple tree are perfectly formed like dark green boiled sweets.

As I walk into the meadows the elder flowers are all out and indeed some are over but it always amazes me that they stagger their flowering and fruiting, to give the insects longer to pollinate them and the birds longer to eat them. There are clumps of purple mallow in the meadow itself. The grass is about 5ft high. Going back to the path I notice that the candles from the horse chestnut are now beginning to form into prickly green conker houses. Above me the meadow lark is singing.

The corn cockles and oxeye daisies in the wild flower patches, planted by the Friends are flowering and there are many plantains this year. The poppies too are in evidence although not at their best in the evening. Miraculously, the seats, made by the Friends out of poplar are beginning to grow.

Moving along the path towards the allotment there are huge hedges of blackberry bramble with startling white flowers. The bramble is so tall as to be over my head, but the bramble is softened by the flowers. I walk down the tall green corridor to find the willow now in blossom near the ash, with its keys like bunches of bananas.

The bryony is in flower on the allotment fence. The umbellifers that flank the river are almost giant in proportion; the pink of the hogweed stands out from the rest. Pineapple mayweed flanks the BMX track and as I hear the rumble of a train I look across to where pylons intersect the A33 Relief Road as they march across the meadows.

The BMX track and the mini hills beyond rustle with russet dock seeds as the wind blows through them. The horseradish has gone to seed but there are still some flowers in existence and this season's tansy is showing fresh bursts of green optimism. I cut through the mini hills to the stream. The hoary cress has gone to seed but the dog rose is in full bloom and the purple comfrey is still in flower, although its flowers are a little raggy, tinged by brown. The stinging nettles are quite predominant and if you look carefully you can see a few orange humps of ladybird larvae cemented to the leaves. The stingers too are going to seed. Bramble blossom lines the path but the stream is quite green and dark

The river is light and airy by comparison and where you can reach its banks you are rewarded by seeing yellow water lilies and water forget-me-not. A tern is fishing, showing us its graceful flight pattern. A corn bunting chirrups exultantly in the weeping willow by the dipping platform. I walk along the path towards Rose Kiln Lane. The burdock is beginning to unfold much to dog walkers annoyance. A tiny green and yellow moth flutters amongst the docks and the chafer beetle with its new found clumsy flight hares around recklessly bashing into everything in its way.

end of July

End of July

The Children's centre is a blaze of colour with a mixture of wild and ornamental flowers. The sunflowers stand tall in the seasonal garden. There are poppies and roses along with corncockles and white campion and a beautiful show of toadflax combined with a good selection of herbs.

The hay in the meadow has been cut and so the river is much more visible, but the meadows now look like the hot summer plains of Africa. The wildflower scrapes are islands of green. The indomitable pineapple mayweed is still fighting its way through the gravel path. There are many people down at the meadows tonight. There is a pale moon over this early evening.

The blackberry thicket is really tall, shrouded in white convolvulus and interspersed with purple thistles. There are wood pigeons roosting in the trees. As I go nearer to the river bank I am delighted to see the native flowering rush much more in evidence along the banks this year.

The BMX track and surrounding area is thick with yellow tansy and stinking goose. In the distance a kestrel is circling. There is a good deal of dock, red in its seedy state, and there is a beautiful sunset beyond the pylons and the A33 Relief road. There are goldfinches among the bramble.

Towards the stream a large area has been razed to the ground by fire and the dust that blows off it looks like wisps of smoke around the black skeletal brambles. I catch a glimpse of what I think is a whitethroat amongst the smoky brambles.

As I approach the stream I see the most beautiful grey heron, at really close range. I move a little closer and it does not fly away, but stays quite still, moving only now and then to paddle further upstream to the bridge. I meet a dog walker and we exchange pleasantries whilst marvelling at the heron; the man's companion, a doberman had dipped in the stream last week and the tan bits of him turned sticky black with oil; an oil change down the drain perhaps? The heron is so still that it attracts little attention from the doberman.

I move along past the kissing gate. The river is teaming with life with darter and chaser dragonflies flit amongst the purple loosestrife and the meadowsweet. Occasionally I see blue and green damsel flies and a beautiful insect that looks as if it has the Devil's finger print on its wings as it flies with a jumping motion. The grasses are tall and golden.

The thistles are going to seed and the down floats past me in the wind. I see yet more goldfinches and as I walk up the overgrown path towards the bridge a thrush rushes out from the undergrowth, grabs a snail and rushes on again. The burdock is coming into flower, and stands against a background of greater willow herb.

I walk back towards the kissing gate where there is flowering reed in abundance. The finches are having a field day with the thistles, pecking at the seed. A boat comes by, clearly making haste to moor up before sundown. The cracked willow lives up to its name, having shed a large branch into the stream.

It is clear that Autumn is just around the corner; the elderberries are ripe, the sloes are set and the haws hang green on the hawthorn. The comfrey is half in flower and half in seed. There is much insect life on the river including the false water boatmen and the fish are biting.

As I approach the dipping platform I see the reeds moving vigorously, and curious, I approach to see what is happening. I see the large body of the heron and it looks as if it is burrowing in the bank. I cannot for the life of me understand this behaviour, for surely it is not typical of a heron. As I get nearer I realise that the heron is dead and is being dragged by its neck through the reeds by what looks to be a mink, a large black furred animal with a fairly long thin tail. I cannot believe my eyes at the horror of the nature before me. Sickened by the loss I cut short my journey and return to the Centre to tell the others what has happened.

end of August

End of August

There is much long golden grass where it hasn't been cut. As I approach the children's centre I see lavatera and buddleia in beautiful flower and the Russian vine that covers the fence is full of its fluffy white flowers. The children's garden is full of interest. As it is evening, the evening primroses are all out ready to attract the night flying insects with their bright yellow radar dish flowers. The sunflowers are heavy with seed and hang their heads. Plantains poke their heads through the wood chip but the ground cover is clearly successful in keeping away most weeds.

The toadflax is looking magnificent as is the dead nettle and the bladder campion and the poppies, too, are holding their own despite the late season. A branch is broken from one of the buddleia trees showing the desire most children have to climb trees. Luckily the buddleia is quite forgiving and its scars will soon heal. In pride of place, newly completed, is a magnificent dragon fly created by the Friends of Waterloo Meadow and the Children's centre out of broken china and set in a circle of concrete. It stands out amongst the woodchip.

I walk on into the meadows. Where the grass has been cut it is lush and green and only the wildflower scrapes are left, brown and seedy in their 'mellow fruitfulness' ready to set seed for next year. Some of the seed has already been gathered by The Friends. The pineapple mayweed is misnamed; it has lasted for most of the summer and still edges the gravel path. There is much yarrow in the meadow and its blooms hover above its stalks like clouds on the meadow.

The sycamore wings hang heavy on the tree, crowded on each stem. There are a few brave umbellifers still with us and some are skeletal like broken umbrellas. The grasshoppers are chirping as if practising for the last night of the proms for the natural world. There are lots of airborne insects everywhere, midges and gnats mainly.

It is good to see that the blackberries are being picked by the people who use the meadows and there are many potential pies in the huge thicket with plenty left for the birds. The haws are now ripe and hang heavy on the tree and the leaves of the hawthorn, as if exhausted by their offspring, turn brown and gold like mature parents.

I pause for a while near the river in a little clearing made by fishermen. Here there are pink umbellifers and the luminiferous red berries of the bittersweet with its potato-like flowers. The tall swords of the burr reed stand to attention in the water. The water lilies float on the river. Perhaps the river is getting cleaner year by year? The willows drape themselves over the water.

The allotment fence is always a good marker of the seasons; the hops hang green like gaudy ear rings in amongst the Virginia creeper and the bryony fights for a place in amongst all this with its half flowers, half berries. It cannot seem to make up its mind which season to be in and reflects how we dress at this time of year, not sure whether to don the winter clothes but wanting to hang onto the summer ones for as long as possible. The tansy is in flower and looks fresh and new with its golden flowers. There are apples on the crab tree and the sun is setting between the tower blocks of Southcote.

The fact that the new Safeway is just around the corner is marked by a shopping trolley in the river. The river by the dipping platform is littered with some beer cans, a margarine container and some old fishing bait. Further on the river is bestrewn by a whole batch of mars ice-cream wrappers. There are many airborne insects on the river tonight, so much so that the fish are jumping (well doing small leaps to break the surface). The burdock is in fine form along the edge of the path; spiky dog terrors abound in the form of their bristly burrs.

I make my way back to the stream. Without the horrors of last month I take my time. The wildflowers by the allotment fence are spectacular, particularly the poppies. I clamber down towards the stream which trickles in the dark thicket before I make my way up towards Makro. At the top of the path there is a beautiful curtain of weeping willow over the stream which itself is marred by a Makro trolley. I head for home out onto the moonscape that is the Makro car park.

End of September

The rowan berries are ripe as we approach the centre. The ash keys are brown and the haws are ripe. The Russian vine on the fence of the children's centre has the appearance of Father Christmas's beard. There are a whole host of parents and toddlers using the fishing platform and the new picnic area with prams and pushchairs.

The leaves are on the turn. The field maple is yellow and brown but the willow is only just beginning to go yellow. I see a dragonfly as I move towards the meadow. There is a Makro trolley in the river near the black berry thicket. The cracked willow branch houses green algae, two tyres, two gas cylinders and 7 plastic bottles in addition to a moorhen fishing. The Virginia creeper on the allotment fence is a beautiful red. The hop fruits are brown. The bryony is only just about able to hold its own. The grasshoppers are chirping. The nettles and umbellifers are in seed. The birds are having a field day with the elder berries on the allotment. The sun is now setting between the tower blocks of Southcote and the Thames Water Plant.

The stream is travelling much quicker and there are clouds of mosquitoes over the river and its banks. The crane flies look like fairies on the side of the stream. The mink I saw last time I wrote is scurrying along the banks of the drainage ditch although again I only see the back of it.

end of October

End of October

Everything looks very autumnal now. Many haws from the hawthorn have been eaten as I approach the centre. The rook's nests are high in the tree. A pair of swans fly over and I can hear the waft waft squeak of their wings. The grass in the meadow is green and short, restored by the cooler weather and more frequent rain. A few lone umbellifers still exist.

The leaves on the trees are red green and brown. The blackberries are now brown husks. There are puddles on the gravel path. The ash keys are brown, like scrunched up paper. There is much less cover by the banks of the river and so the river is much more visible. There is a branch of cracked willow in the river which is still collecting rubbish. Some of the convolvulus has nearly climbed to the top of the willow trees.

The hops and bryony are just brown ropes now, hanging on the allotment fence. The sun is setting very near to the Thames Water Plant. There are still specks of yellow tansy amongst the green of the BMX track. A small willow near the BMX track still has many green leaves. It is interesting to notice how the trees all turn different colours at different rates.

The stream is running quite fast. The vegetative cover on its bank has died back considerably. There are several ducks and moorhens on the river. There is a lone juvenile swan looking for bread and looking disappointed to find I have none. The cracked willow branch in the river houses a shopping trolley, an old oil drum and a tyre. The thicket of small trees which housed violets in the spring is carpeted with brown leaves and cans! There are many blue sloes on the blackthorn. There is a very clear panorama of the bridge and of the opposite bank which is just as denuded as this one, but the lack of leaves on the trees is due mainly to high winds rather than cold weather. The alders by the river are laden with cones which will provide much food for the birds in the coming months.

There is a mist on the stream which hangs like a cataract and is so visible as to be almost tangible. The starlings are beginning their roosting behaviour, swirling and twisting in unison as if by remote control.

enð of November

End of November

We are now leaving the end of Autumn and it is the beginning of Winter. There are just a few straggly berries left on the hawthorn as I approach the meadows. The bird table in the children's garden has food on it and there's one single rose left on the rose bush with a few Autumnal leaves hanging on to the shrubs. The sky is raked with pink today as the sun is beginning to set.

Around the base of the sycamore, the once beautiful Autumn leaves lay stranded in a colourful carpet of yellow and russet and brown as if paying tribute to the ghostly tree from which they came. Further on, the ash keys hang in abundant clumps like ghostly bats in a foreign country. Surprisingly the bramble is still quite green although it has served as a rubbish trap and there are bits and pieces of rubbish wound round the thorns. The oak still has many of its leaves but they are ochre in colour making poetic alliteration. There are a few leaves hanging on for grim death on the crab

90

apple. The willow on the BMX track has leaves of brown and green that rustle in the wind.

The reeds in the reed beds near the BMX track still have their flowers and their fluffy blossom is rustling in the wind; it is a 'coffee with milk' colour. The russet of the dock flowers contrasts with the yellow of the tansy; these look surprisingly fresh, probably as a result of the fire earlier on in the year.

I move on towards the stream. It is looking dark and grey and black. There is much dying vegetation on the sides of its bank. The banks are bestrewn with litter which once was camouflaged but is now ostentatious and catches the eye.

The hawthorns past the kissing gate still have some berries, but the elder, previously laden with fruit has been stripped bare by the birds. As I move further on towards Rose Kiln Lane the sun is setting and I am suddenly aware of how the blackthorn gets its name for it is possibly the darkest silhouette on the sky line, easily the blackest tree around. The area past the kissing gate is usually impenetrable but the vegetation has died back to such an extent that the whole area looks more open and field-like. The silhouettes of the burdock stand out to look like trees.

End of December

The temperatures today are some of the coldest for the year and in addition to this winds from Siberia are so chilling so as to make it feel even colder. The hawthorn on the approach to the meadows is providing shelter for many blue tits and tree sparrows who are clearly visible through the twigs and branches and are much more precocious than usual, clearly being more concerned with keeping warm rather than flying away; they puff their feathers up almost in unison.

The beech is providing food for many birds today and imagine my surprise to see *two* pairs of goldfinches eating from the mast. The bird table at the children's centre is well-stocked and well-visited by a whole host of birds.

Overhead I see many black-headed gulls spiralling and wheeling in the icy thermals. A small flock of starlings are beginning their roosting behaviour, twisting and turning in formation, nearing a tree as if to land and then veering away at the last minute before finding their roost in the long grasses near the river. The blackberry bramble is still surprisingly green and is showing the silver underside of its leaves.

The river is much more visible than usual, much of the vegetation having died and in addition to this the river is higher and wider. The cracked willow branch which usually hosts an array of litter has shed its load due to the rise in water levels and is sheltering instead a mallard duck and drake. As I stand and watch, two pairs of swans use the river as their runway and take off to go further towards town and I can hear the soft waft waft squeak of their wings before I see their huge bodies fly overhead.

The sun is now setting to the left of the Thames Water Plant creating a magnificent sunset of pinks and mauves and grey clouds with silver linings. It is too cold to linger today. Any part of my body that has not been covered, has frozen and I follow the path back the way I came. You might be forgiven for thinking that the meadows would look dull and grey and black on such a cold winter's day but my diligence has been rewarded with a spectrum of colours in this urban nature reserve.

end of January

End of January

The children's centre garden has been cleared by FOWM and looks very tidy. There are buds on the buddleia. I walk across the meadows from the children's centre garden to the gravel path. On the way I see four pieces of dog mess. Without the covering of the long grass one can clearly see the undulating shape of the land which was once a land fill site.

A musty damp wood smell pervades. The odd brave gnat has ventured out today, the weather being fairly mild. The umbellifers of the previous season look skeletal and shrouded in the brown cobwebs of dying vegetation but are cheered up by the rosy glow of the late afternoon sun. The cracked willow branch in the river is only sheltering a small amount of sludge due to the raised water level and a coot is fishing.

The short winter grass is green and pale ochre in colour. Following the winter equinox the sun is beginning its journey back in the sky and is now setting slightly to the right of the Thames Water Plant.

Before I reach the kissing gate I see a small group of female chaffinches in a large alder. I see a sudden flash of blue as I walk towards Rose Kiln Lane; an overwintering kingfisher has clearly found enough food to sustain it, even in the coldest of weather. The denuded trees reveal a tiny nest, now vacated, that was not visible to me previously but is a marvel of bird engineering.

Further along in the river there is the inevitable Indesit gas bottle, several plastic bottles and two shopping trolleys. From the last alder before Rose Kiln Lane I can see a wide panorama of the river which is usually closed to view when the vegetation returns. The clouds in this winter sky have a pink lining to them as the sun sets.

It is a fairly mild afternoon and the song thrush is defending its territory with its beautiful song as if it was a fine spring day; it is answered by a song thrush from across the river. A pair of magpies are playing around in the field maples as I leave the meadows.

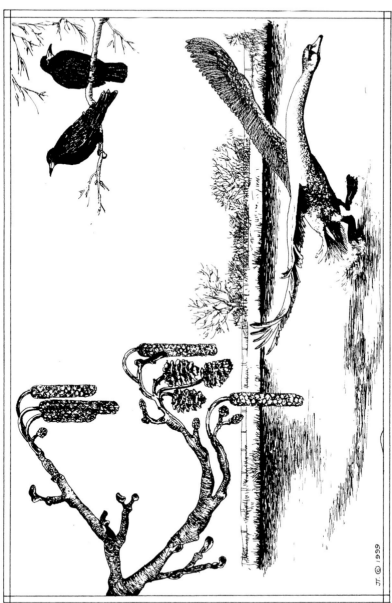

end of February

JT. © 1999

End of February

It is one of the coldest Februarys on record. It is so cold that I can hardly bear to take my hands out of my pocket to write. It is 5 below zero and the wind is bitter. It is very quiet almost because of the cold. There is a sense of waiting; waiting for something to happen. The white poplar welcomes me to the meadow with its fluffy buds. The pussy willow near the river has pollen on it. The Russian Vine is alive with green spurs. There are the green shoots of daffodils in the small copse near the children's centre. There are two lone rooks sitting amongst the alder catkins. I think there is a starling impersonating a telephone in the trees on the opposite bank of the river. I can hear a blackbird singing. The bird life is quite visible given the sparse nature of the vegetation; I can see chaffinches and great tits. It is hard to believe that the last time I was here it was so mild and now it is <u>so</u> cold.

I can see the roving behaviour of siskins as they feed on the alder trees. The river is still visible through the trees, shrouded in the brown of last year's vegetation. A moorhen heads off for the bank as I approach. As I watch the river I see the swan use the river as its runway. This has been a common sight for me at the meadows but I never tire of it. A brave mole has made mole hills on the meadow so the ground must be warming up, albeit slowly. In the distance I notice the cracked willows. They are green with shoots and this offers hope that spring is nearly here.

end of March

JT. © 1999

98

End of March

Last time I was here there were just a few clues that Spring was on its way but this time there is no mistake. The daffodils in the children's centre garden are out and there are primroses in the bath tub of the 'bog' garden. There are a pair of doves eating grain under the bird table. Everywhere is very clear after the Kennet clean-up which takes place in March each year. The blackthorn blossom is out and the leaves are beginning to shoot. The hawthorn is in full leaf. There is blossom on the crab apple. The elder has shoots on it and even at this stage there are the very beginnings of the berries amongst it. The place is alive with bird song.

There are a host of dandelion clocks, and the inevitable dock and bramble by the path. Some new cracked willows are growing near the stream. There are quite a few midges. There are brown ash keys still hanging on the branches even though the tree has its black buds. The usual land marks of debris in the river are gone, demolished by the river clean-up.

The rustic seat near the BMX track has been bitten at by animals of the human kind; at least it's evidence of use. The celandine is out, mistaken by some as the buttercup but that comes later. There has been much clearance work to make way for the SUSTRANS route. This is a cycle route that will spread the length and breadth of Britain by the year 2000. One could be forgiven for thinking that this is environmental vandalism when one sees trees shorn off in their prime but although the work could have been carried out more sensitively I suppose we have to look forwards for the greater environmental good.

The blackthorn thicket looks like a maze of snow storm; the blossom is really busy and wild. The violets in the blackthorn thicket are sadly over; tune in next spring for another amazing viewing. As I leave the river and the meadows I see a heron flying overhead as if looking for something and then circling and following the same route again. It looks almost prehistoric, like a pterodactyl, as if it has been around since the dinosaurs and I reflect that I hope it, along with all the other wonders I have seen, will not go the same way.

The final instalment

The elderflowers are just out. cow parsley is in blossom and marks the start of a long stream of umbellifers that will flower in succession all through the season; the hogweed is just about to come out. The SUSTRANS path is amazing. The path looks as if it has been in the meadows all the time. The indomitable mallow is green and abundant. The meadow grass is very green and very long, bedecked occasionally with buttercups.

The sycamore copters are already formed and although Summer isn't even with us yet we are reminded that time moves fast and in the midst of Spring we are already getting a preview of Autumn. There is blossom on the horse chestnut tree. The wildflower scrapes are a profusion of oxeye daisies and greater plantains. The stinging nettles are really tall. The oak is in full leaf now, its blossom is over. The bryony is in flower. The apples on the crab apple tree are beginning to set.

The stream is running clear and fast and there are minnows in it. The stream is flanked by an abundance of hedge garlic which is in flower. The hawthorn blossom is over and the haws are beginning to set. The comfrey is in flower. I get excited as I see some pink on the far bank of the river but through my binoculars I identify it as a discarded bait tin. A common tern is fishing in the river and making amazing flight patterns as if to give me my own private aeronautics display. Although everything in the meadows is tall and verdant the reeds that line the river are still green and short. The docks are in seed and very tall. The pond area that was created in the meadows by Thames water is beginning to be colonized by hoary cress, comfrey and bramble.

It is fitting that I should leave the meadows in the middle of Spring, just as I had found them the previous year. The notes for winter indicate the ending of the year but the notes for spring signify the beginning and that would be my best hope for this book; that it signifies the beginning of something rather than the end. Just as a new day signifies hope, vitality and energy so a new season does the same. This is why we saw the book as a Sunrise over Waterloo Meadows.

Bibliography

Title	Author	Publisher	Year
The Growth of Reading	Edited by Malcolm Petyt. Contributors: Cecil Slade, Brian Kemp, Tony Corley, Joan Dils	Alan Sutton Publishing Ltd	1993
Berkshire in the War Vol. 1	Reading Standard Pictorial Record		1916
Reading at War	Stuart Hylton	Alan Sutton Publishing Ltd in conjunction with Reading Chronicle	1996
Coley: Portrait of an Urban Village	Phoebe Cusden	Reading branch of The Workers' Educational Association	1977
Reading 70 years ago	P. H. Ditchfield		
Co-op literature	The Co-op	The Co-op	1996
Article by Leslie North	Leslie North	Reading Chronicle	29 Aug 1980
Windows into the past	Wynne Frankum	Katesgrove School Room	
Christchurch School – A short account of the work and activities of the school, from its foundation to the present day. 1868-1968	G. M. Luxton		
R100 article		Daily Mail	6 Oct 1930
A History of Education in Reading (unpublished dissertation thesis)	L. W. Harman	Reading University	1960
Men of the period	The Biographical Publishing Company	Berkshire Record Office	